How to Talk About

Places You've Never Been

ALSO BY PIERRE BAYARD

Sherlock Holmes Was Wrong
How to Talk About Books You Haven't Read

How to Talk About

Places You've Never Been

On the Importance of
Armchair Travel

PIERRE BAYARD

Translated by Michele Hutchison

B L O O M S B U R Y

NEW YORK · LONDON · OXFORD · NEW DELHI · SYDNEY

Bloomsbury USA
An imprint of Bloomsbury Publishing Plc

1385 Broadway   50 Bedford Square
New York   London
NY 10018   WC1B 3DP
USA   UK

www.bloomsbury.com

BLOOMSBURY and the Diana logo are trademarks of Bloomsbury
Publishing Plc

First published 2016

ISBN: HB: 978-1-62040-137-8
         ePub: 978-1-62040-138-5

LIBRARY OF CONGRESS CATALOGING-IN-PUBLICATION DATA HAS BEEN
APPLIED FOR.

2 4 6 8 10 9 7 5 3 1

Typeset by RefineCatch Limited, Bungay, Suffolk

Printed and bound in USA by Berryville Graphics Inc., Berryville, Virginia

To find out more about our authors and books visit www.bloomsbury.com.
Here you will find extracts, author interviews, details of forthcoming
events and the option to sign up for our newsletters.

Bloomsbury books may be purchased for business or promotional use. For
information on bulk purchases please contact Macmillan Corporate and
Premium Sales Department at specialmarkets@macmillan.com.

A History of Nebraska *by Clinton York. The author was a gentleman about forty-seven who said he had never been to Nebraska but he had always been interested in the state.*

"Ever since I was a child it's been Nebraska for me. Other kids listened to the radio or raved on about their bicycles. I read everything I could find on Nebraska. I don't know what got me started on the thing. But, any way, this is the most complete history ever written about Nebraska."

The book was in seven volumes and he had them in a shopping bag when he came into the library.

—RICHARD BRAUTIGAN, *The Abortion: An Historical Romance 1966*

Contents

Procedures to Follow   *115*

List of Abbreviations

op. cit.	*opere citato*, in the work cited
ibid.	*ibidem*, in the same place
UP	unknown place
VP	visited place
DP	discussed place
FP	forgotten place
++	very positive review
+	positive review
−	negative review
−−	very negative review

Prologue

THE INCONVENIENCES OF TRAVEL have been sufficiently enough studied for me to not linger on the subject. Ill-equipped to defend itself against wild animals, inclement weather or illness, the human body is clearly not made for leaving its usual habitat and even less so for traveling to lands far removed from those where God intended us to live.

To these natural elements over which the human being has little control, we must add the unpleasantness man causes with his own ill conduct. Contrary to the dreams of certain utopians, the world is no safer now than it was in the past and, being fortunate enough to live in a relatively sheltered place, I have difficulty understanding the reasons that might lead me to leave it and risk facing hard knocks on hostile soil.

But the dangers of travel do not stop here. By focusing too much on the physical inconveniences, you lose sight of the psychological disturbances it can cause. We know from Freud and the works of other psychiatrists who have studied the various travelers' syndromes that traveling a long way from home is not only liable to provoke psychiatric problems, it can also drive you mad.[1]

All of these inconveniences would not be sufficient to keep me at home if there were not an extra consideration—in my eyes, the deciding factor. It can be found at the heart of this book. There is actually nothing to show that traveling *is* the best way to discover a town or a country you do not know. Everything points to the contrary—and the experience of numerous writers supports this—if you want to be able to talk about a place, the best thing to do is stay at home.

∾

It is necessary to be very specific and dispel any ambiguity up front. If this book joins a long line of books denouncing the harmful effects of travel, it is not because it shares the sentiment of numerous authors that, all places being equal, there is no need to go to the trouble of leaving home and discovering any of them.

This theory was popularized by a well-known poem by Baudelaire, "The Voyage"—which includes the line "Bitter is the knowledge gained in traveling"—and in which the poet develops the theory that visiting foreign countries only leads to boredom and, once the journey is over, leaves the traveler confronted with the terrifying void of his own personality.

My own thoughts are radically different. Contrary to

---

1. For different forms of travelers' syndrome see in particular Graziella Magherini's *La sindrome di Stendhal* (Milan: Ponte alle Grazie, 1989) and Régis Airault's *Fous de l'Inde: Délires d'Occidentaux et sentiment océanique* (Paris: Éditions Payot & Rivages, 2002).

Baudelaire, whose ideas are imbued with some kind of Eurocentrism and in any case fail to demonstrate any great intellectual curiosity, I have found all of the countries and the cultures I have ever had the opportunity to encounter greatly enriching, and I have never regretted making the effort to interest myself in them.

Therefore, the question is not what we can gain from a knowledge of foreign places—acquaintance with which can only be beneficial to anyone with an open mind—it is to know whether this acquaintance should take place directly or whether it isn't wiser to practice it through means other than physical travel.

∾

This book is therefore dedicated to an essayistic figure I will refer to as the armchair traveler. Unlike Baudelaire, this individual does not believe that all cultures lead us back to ourselves. Both unconcerned with taking risks and wanting to keep a safe distance from the object of his research, he is capable of separating physical travel from mental displacement and takes care to limit his movements as much as possible.

Primarily concerned here are autobiographical writers who have described in minute detail places they have never visited, something that has not prevented them from issuing protracted diatribes on their subjects and rendering them—thanks to the power of their writing—more present than those described by writers who considered traveling to them essential.

But writers are not the only ones this book will cover. For various reasons, such as a fear of danger or the feeling that a trip wouldn't be worthwhile, a whole series of essayists, by

trade or in passing—anthropologists, journalists, athletes—
have been compelled at certain moments in their lives to
describe places they have never seen.

Apart from these specific cases, we will see that, more
frequently than one might expect, there are situations in
daily life—from adultery to theft to murder—when the
practice of lying about the place you were at a particular
moment can turn out to be of great utility, or even prove
crucial to your safety or survival.

∼

Aside from offering practical advice, this book, if it engages in
a reflection on armchair travel and ways of behaving in society
when forced to talk about places we have never visited, also
aims to reflect on the relationship between literature and the
world it portrays and, in particular, the places it hosts.

The fact that writers and many essayists, when placed in
situations where they find themselves compelled to create
fictions, manage to render unknown places realistically and
give them a plausible form of existence effectively poses the
question: what kind of space is posited in literature and how
is it accommodated in language?

In order to reflect on this particular relationship between
literature and space, the act of description, to which writers
have frequent recourse in their daily practice, is key, because
it provides a privileged observation post for studying the
singularities of the fictional space that literature invents and
the significant differences between it and the real world.

Beyond this matter of the literary space or topos, these

discursive fictions open up the question of truth in literature. Concurrent with scientific truth about places borne
out by geography, there is a different kind of truth about the
world that is revealed by armchair travelers—one that
doesn't imply physical travel and whose operating instruc-
tions this book will endeavor to identify.

∽

A logical structure emerges from these general considerations. In the first part of the book, I will review the different types of nonjourneys that a whole succession of writers
and thinkers, unconcerned with moving away from their
home turf, have employed in order to encounter the foreign
cultures they wish to know and describe.

In the second part, I will describe a number of concrete
situations in which we might find ourselves forced to talk
about places we have never been to. These situations are
actually much more numerous than one thinks, hence the
interest in examining them with care and studying them
separately, attentive to their individual complexities and the
range of solutions they call for.

In the third section, based on my personal experiences
but also on those of numerous other armchair travelers, I
will offer several pieces of practical advice to those who,
desirous of encountering foreign cultures, have understood
that running around the world at their own risk is not the
best way to go about enriching their minds.

∽

This is the logical sequel to my previous book, *How to Talk About Books You Haven't Read*. Both are concerned with using concrete situations in life to demonstrate that our partial or total ignorance of a subject need not necessarily prove a handicap to an appropriate discussion about it and can even be used to improve our knowledge of the world.

As in the previous work, and for the sake of intellectual honesty, for each important place cited by an author or myself, I will indicate in a footnote my exact degree of knowledge, or more likely ignorance, of the place. And, convinced that it is not necessary to displace oneself physically to gain an accurate view of the world, I will not shy away from expressing my personal feelings about it each time.

This is the way of Immanuel Kant, a man who never deviated from the route of his daily walk nor ventured very far from his birthplace of Königsberg, Prussia, a fact that did not in the least prevent him from describing or commenting on foreign parts.[2] Naturally this book is dedicated to that classic example of the armchair traveler.

---

2. "That Kant was very serious about improving his mind power is demonstrated by the fact that he introduced and taught a course on physical geography at the university. He was also a passionate reader of all kinds of travel journals and—for someone who had never left Königsberg—he would have been able to find his way just as well around London as Italy. He said that he didn't have time to travel precisely because he wanted to know just as much about a great number of countries." Hannah Arendt, *Lectures on Kant's Political Philosophy* (Chicago: University of Chicago Press, 1992). Peter Szendy comments on this quote in *Kant chez les extraterrestres: Philosofictions cosmopolitiques* (Paris: Les Éditions de Minuit, 2011).

Various Ways of Not Traveling

Places You Don't Know

(in which we learn that Marco Polo's accounts are
of great scientific value to the study of griffin and
unicorn behavior)

THERE ARE FEW NAMES in the history of travel as glorious and symbolic as that of Marco Polo. Even more than Christopher Columbus and Vasco da Gama, his name is linked to the idea of adventure and the discovery of unknown lands. He practically epitomizes the association of physical courage with knowledge.

Our private hearing of Marco Polo does not only take into account the journeys he made and his long sojourns abroad but also the particularly well-documented accounts he left behind. It is these, passed down through the centuries by scrupulous copyists, that, being firsthand, give us exceptional insights into the medieval Asiatic world and in particular the Chinese empire, which was largely unknown to the West before Marco Polo arrived and lived there awhile.

≈

The life of Marco Polo, a Venetian merchant who lived from 1254 to 1324, was an extraordinary adventure. He was fifteen when his father and uncle, traveling merchants from Venice, returned from a long voyage in central Asia where they had met the Mongolian emperor Kublai Khan, grandson of Genghis Khan, who had given them a letter for the pope.

Two years later, Marco accompanied them when they returned to China[1] and discovered Kublai Khan's court for himself. He entered into service with the Mongolian emperor and, charged with various missions in China and other Asian countries, he took on increasingly important functions at court. This gave him an exceptionally broad overview of the Chinese empire and its management, as well as of its neighboring countries.

Gone from his native country for more than twenty years, Polo returned after long peregrinations, and, thanks to a fortune accumulated in China, he went on to arm a galley in order to fight in the war taking place between Venice and Genoa. He was taken prisoner during a naval battle and incarcerated in Genoa; this was where he dictated an account of his travels to a fellow captive, the writer Rustichello da Pisa.

The original text, most likely written in 1298 in Old French, has not reached us, but numerous editions were in circulation in the Middle Ages, and these can give us a clear enough impression of its form and content. Today these editions allow us to access Marco Polo's fabulous travels with as much of a sense of wonder as his first readers had.

---

1. UP--

~

Marco Polo's contribution is actually of vital importance to gaining a complete picture of medieval Asia. He left behind accurate information about all the countries, regions and towns he passed through and described them one by one, from the Middle East to Japan, reviewing the customs of the inhabitants, geography, currency, agriculture and religion.

His information is all the more significant because it takes the form of an objective, systematic account. Whatever the town or country he passed through, Marco Polo stopped to fill in a comprehensive report, taking great care to note down any factual or scientific information that might be needed by anyone deciding to follow in his footsteps.

The country he covered the most comprehensively was China. He lived there for seventeen years and knew it through and through. His book is particularly rich in information on the imperial capital and its fortifications, on the palace of the great khan, the Mongolian army and its composition, on the distribution of command posts or surprise tactics—one of which was pretending to flee—all of which allowed the Mongols to triumph over their enemies.

He goes into just as much detail about the Mongolian admin-istration. Marco Polo was employed there for a long time and describes its workings exhaustively. The reader learns how the empire was divided up into twelve administrative districts, how mail circulated around the whole empire between the capital and the provinces via a sophisticated messenger relay system, how the empire protected the population from epidemics or famine and which technical processes were used to mint money.

But Marco Polo's input isn't only important for the knowledge it provides on the army or the imperial government. His work also comprises a wealth of well-underpinned information on everyday China and daily life there, from religious practices and celebrations to clothing and food.

∽

Marco Polo's work offers us a unique firsthand account of the amorous customs of the inhabitants of the countries he traveled through or stayed in. Its power derives both from its narrative quality and the original information it provides.

This is particularly the case in the area around Xichang— Marco Polo gives us an unembellished report of the sexual habits of its inhabitants:

> I would like to add that, in this region, there is a custom I will tell you about concerning people's wives. The menfolk do not consider it a disgrace when a stranger or another person dishonors their wife, their daughter, their sister or any other woman in their household; they consider it a great blessing for them to be bedded and they say that, thanks to this, their gods and idols are better disposed and give them an abundance of the riches of this world.[2]

---

2. *La description du monde* [*The Travels of Marco Polo*] (Paris: Le Livre de poche, 1998), 281. English translation by Michele Hutchison.

This is how we learn that when welcoming a stranger into their home, the inhabitants of Xichang order their wives to satisfy their guest's every whim and fancy and then voluntarily leave the house and don't come back until the stranger, who might have spent three or four days there, has left. During this time, the stranger has been able to freely avail himself of all the women living there:

> This is why they give their wives with such generosity to strangers and other people, as I told you. Note that when they see that a stranger is looking for a place to stay, everybody is glad and happy to invite them into their homes and, once he is installed, the master of the house goes out immediately and orders his wife to satisfy all the stranger's desires forthwith. Then, once he has given the command, he goes out to his vineyards or his fields and doesn't return until the stranger has left. Hence the stranger sometimes stays three or four days in the poor devil's home, having a good time with his wife, his daughter, his sister or whoever he chooses.[3]

To ensure that his satisfaction is complete, it is important to avoid disturbing the stranger in his pleasures. The inhabitants of Xichang invented an information system of great simplicity that afforded their guests the necessary peace and tranquillity:

> While he is staying there, the stranger's hat is hung from the window or the door or some other signal is given so

---

3. Ibid.

that the master of the house knows that the other man is still there: as long as the sign is there, he will not dare return. This custom is practiced across the entire region.[4]

The Xichang region, however, is not the only part of China where travelers are offered such sexual hospitality. The same goes for Tibet, where a woman's value is proportionate to the number of partners she has had before marriage. This functions as an incentive for the women to offer themselves to any overnight guests, going so far as to collect souvenirs so as to be able to prove the intensity of their sex lives to their future husbands:

> The woman with the most medals and trinkets who can show she has been touched the most is considered the best, and a man marries her with the greatest pleasure because it is said that she is the luckiest.[5]

Of great interest, we learn, for its unexpected revelations about the hospitality and sexual customs of locals, *The Travels of Marco Polo* is equally fascinating for the descriptions it offers of the fauna of the places traversed, of which the book provides incomparable descriptions in scientific terms.

---

4. It is a country of dreams in many other realms too—gold flows there: "And this is the inhabitant's currency. They have gold ingots and weigh them on sets of scales; the ingots' value is related to their weight, but they don't have any coinage" (ibid.).

5. Ibid., 277. The Tibet in question doesn't correspond to today's Tibet but to the mountainous part of Sichuan.

This applies to the passage dedicated to portraying animals on the island of Java, in particular the unicorn, whose exact nature has fueled debates since antiquity before being definitively established by Marco Polo, who puts an end to the legendary representations:

They have great numbers of elephants and also great numbers of unicorns, which are not much smaller than the elephants. Here is what they look like: they have the same hide as a buffalo, feet like an elephant, and they have very thick, black horns in the middle of their foreheads. The unicorn does not injure with its horn but with its tongue since it has lengthy spines on its tongue. It has the head of a wild boar and always carries its head pointing downward. It likes to dwell in lakes and bogs. It is a very ugly creature, not the kind one could capture with the breast of a young virgin as they say at home: no, quite the contrary.[6]

Just as instructive in scientific terms is the description of Andaman Island, whose inhabitants have certain morphological features that were revealed only by Marco Polo:

Andaman is a very large island. Its people don't have a king, they are idolatrous and are veritable wild beasts. I should add that the men on this island of Andaman have dogs' heads, their teeth and eyes too: their faces perfectly resemble large mastiffs. They have large quantities of

---

6. Ibid., 397.

spices, they are very cruel because they eat everything they can catch as long as it is not their own kind.[7]

And the same applies to the island of Mogadishu and certain of its creatures, about which the traveling merchant provides crucial information:

The griffin is so strong it seizes an elephant with its talons, lifts it up very high then drops it again, breaking the elephant's bones, then the griffin sits on top and eats its fill. The people of the island call them *rucks*, and they have no other name, so I do not know whether there is a larger bird or whether this bird is a griffin. Still, it does not have the shape we lend to it—half lion, half bird—but is gigantic and resembles the eagle.[8]

We see the extent to which, in terms of the inhabitants' customs but also those of animals, Marco Polo's accounts should be praised for making us change our often overly rigid mental habits and adapt to alternative worlds whose discovery can only serve to enrich us intellectually.

∾

Surprising in what it describes, Marco Polo's work is also surprising in what it fails to describe, as if the narrator's

---

7. Ibid., 405.
8. Ibid., 453.

focus on certain aspects of the countries he visits is bizarrely accompanied by a prudent reserve about others.

First of all, it should be noted that the explorer showed great discretion in China, the country in which he claims to have lived for the longest time. Such great discretion that the imperial archives, which are, moreover, very comprehensive, bear no trace of his passage, despite the fact that he says he was assigned important duties.[9]

Equally astonishing are certain gaps in his account, as though he was suddenly blinded or became distracted at certain moments. It is surprising that someone might describe China for dozens of pages without the slightest mention of the thousands of kilometers of the Great Wall that Marco Polo is supposed to have crossed at several occasions during his peregrinations.

Though he pays attention to the smallest stories, Marco Polo doesn't find anything to say about the bound feet of Chinese women, nor about the tea ceremony, nor cormorant fishing. And generally attentive to the linguistic particularities of the places he visits, he doesn't appear to have noticed the existence of ideograms.

All of these improbabilities have led authors of skeptical persuasion—including the sinologist Frances Wood in *Did Marco Polo Go to China?*—to express certain doubts about the actual presence of Marco Polo in China. Wood comments that the book appears more like an accumulation of records than the account of a real journey, whose stages,

---

9. Frances Wood, *Did Marco Polo Go to China?* (Berkeley: Westview Press, 1998), 132.

moreover, it would be very difficult to reconstruct from the incoherent information offered to us.

Following her reasoning to its logical conclusion, Frances Wood challenges most of Marco Polo's travels, advancing the theory that, in reality, he got no further than Constantinople, where his family had a bar which numerous travelers passed through, their stories feeding his reverie.

∾

Though we usually recognize the acclaim for his courage and the scientific quality of his information, if we consider the evidence, we see that what Marco Polo did possess was a great deal of imagination—a quality insufficiently stressed by critics of his work.[10]

If we consider this Venetian trader, his women offered to all-comers and his men with dogs' heads, the first type of place differentiates itself from all of the types of places we will examine in this book—the place one doesn't know. In fact, it is difficult to believe, given what Marco Polo relates and what he omits to say, that he did actually go to Kublai Khan's China at all.

Might it not actually be that his text powerfully illustrates the important fact that the travelogue is a favorable place for the practice of fiction—since the reality of Polo's travels clearly didn't prevent him from witnessing improbable scenes or being affected by hallucinations sufficiently

---

10. In *Invisible Cities* by Italo Calvino (1972), it is to the Chinese emperor himself, not to westerners, that Marco Polo describes fifty-five imaginary cities.

pervasive that they continued to haunt him during the writing of his account?

These scenes are close to the ones that populate dreams, where sexuality crops up constantly when not directly represented, or composite creatures are produced by condensing images, or an ideal world dominated by infantile omnipotence substitutes, in a kind of narrative euphoria, the depressing everyday reality.[11]

This permanent link between the travelogue and the practice of fiction means that we are placed in a different register of truth than in traditional narratives, which are forced to choose between truth and lies. It is a register where fiction—or at least indecision about the authenticity of the reported facts—is considered to play an active role in the narrative and therefore doesn't shock the reader in the slightest since he accepts the principle.

Actually, it should be noted that this Freudian "other scene" is not an isolated construct but pluralistic. Marco Polo's accounts functioned equally well in his day because they corresponded to an expectation and belonged within a collective imagination where no one was surprised to come across dog-headed men in their readings. And they continue to be received today as credible documents, even though they seem to have been infiltrated by imaginary beings and

---

11. It is no trivial matter that Marco Polo describes the sex lives of the inhabitants of Xichang with such verve. Places you don't know function like dreams or daydreams, offering a privileged space for deploying your unconscious fantasies, allowing repression to be lifted. These are the equivalents of what Freud calls "the other scene," the unconscious.

fantasies. What they help to build therefore is a space for reverie, outside of the constraints of science.

∼

If Marco Polo's travels recall the role that fiction plays in every travelogue, they also question the boundaries between travel and nontravel.

The fact that, centuries after the tribulations of one of the most famous explorers in history, medieval specialists are incapable of coming to an agreement about whether he actually made it to the Far East or whether he wisely remained at home speaks volumes about the difficulty of separating travel from nontravel, and in so doing, the complexity of attempting to grasp the notion of travel with any rigor.

As we'll see in this book, there are many intermediate cases between travel and nontravel—as there are between reading and nonreading—and being in a situation where unknown places are discussed is, in fact, much more common than we think and not limited to the extreme case of travelers remaining in their homes.

This uncertainty about the boundary between travel and nontravel is intimately tied up with the fiction that accompanies any description of a place. The capacity of human beings to imagine things means first and foremost that descriptions linked to real travel should always be nuanced—realizing just how much they are mixed up with personal fantasies, whether the author has intended this or not, and that a traveler is capable of recounting in good faith scenes or imaginary locations he has ended up believing in.

Furthermore, this recognition of the active role of fiction in the travelogue presumably dissuades many potential travelers from traveling. They have become aware of the fact that the essential point is the quality of the reveries produced about the places to be visited, plus the narrative force of their account—a reverie and an account that in order to germinate and grow, won't necessarily gain anything from being founded on an authentic trip.

≈

I have often asked myself where Marco Polo spent the twenty years he disappeared for and what mysterious occupation kept him in the mysterious place he chose as a sanctuary.

I doubt, unlike Frances Wood, that Marco Polo ventured as far as Constantinople. His piecemeal knowledge of China can be explained in quite a different way: in talks he had with travelers returning to Italy. I am more inclined to believe that he chose to retreat to a secluded, peaceful place somewhere near Venice.

And if we run with this theory, how is it impossible to think that it was for the love of a woman that Marco Polo shut himself off from the world for so long—a woman to whom he enjoyed recounting the imaginary travels he invented for her and the purely fictional countries he struggled to cross, braving a thousand deaths in his mind?

2

Places You've Been Through

(in which Jules Verne instructs us on how to travel
without leaving our cabins or abandoning our
critical faculties)

IF IT IS IMPOSSIBLE to stay at home in the company of your
beloved like Marco Polo did, and if you are obliged in spite
of everything to travel, the best solution is to do it as quickly
as possible, avoiding lingering anywhere along the way since
nothing good can come of it.

This rapidity of movement allows you, first of all, to
protect yourself. It is obvious that the risks of unfortunate
accidents, illness or ill-timed encounters with locals or the
local fauna, which don't always have the best of intentions,
are much higher if one stays in a place far from home for a
long period of time.

However, as we will see, rushing through an area as
opposed to visiting it thoroughly is not necessarily a negative act or omission, dictated by considerations of prudence.
Such an approach can also be the primary requirement for

gaining an accurate impression, in which case prudence becomes another name for scientific rigor.

∾

One of the literary characters who best represents the practice of accelerated travel must be Phileas Fogg, the character created by Jules Verne in one of his most famous novels, *Around the World in Eighty Days*.

Jules Verne presents Phileas Fogg as a man whose entire existence is organized around scientific values, starting with punctuality:

> He was so exact that he was never in a hurry, was always ready, and was economical alike of his steps and motions. He never took one step too many, and always went to his destination by the shortest cut; he made no superfluous gestures, and was never seen to be moved or agitated. He was the most deliberate person in the world, yet always reached his destination at the exact moment.
>
> He lived alone, and so to speak, outside of every social relation; and as he knew that in this world account must be taken of friction, and that friction retards, he never rubbed against anybody.[1]

After a wager made in the Reform Club during a discussion on scientific progress, this prim and proper English

---

1. Jules Verne, *Around the World in Eighty Days*, trans. George Makepeace Towle (Boston: James R. Osgood and Company, 1873), 9.

gentleman commits himself to attempting to circumnavigate the earth in less than eighty days. He has promised to pay half of his fortune to the people who have taken the bet if he doesn't manage to accomplish it.

Fogg throws himself into the high-risk venture with a single companion, his French servant Passepartout, whom he has recently hired. He manages somehow to stick to the program he has set himself, but after a number of adventures, and because he is being chased by an English policemen, Fix—who has mistaken him for a malefactor and arrests him when he arrives in England, causing him to lose precious time—he arrives in London a few hours too late.

But Fogg has forgotten something crucial in his calculations. Having traveled around the world in the opposite direction from the sun, he gained an hour when crossing each time zone, and the accumulation of hours saved has given him, by the end of his voyage, a twenty-four-hour bonus. So he hasn't arrived in London a few hours too late, but a few hours too early, and thanks to Passepartout, who discovers what date it actually is by chance, he wins his bet.

∼

Even if he does travel around the planet he is making a complete tour of, Phileas Fogg is adamant that what he is doing does not fall under travel but a way of not traveling.

Fogg is expressly disinterested in the regions he passes through, passing up any form of tourism:

Always the same impassible member of the Reform Club, whom no incident could surprise, as unvarying as the ship's chronometers, and seldom having the curiosity even to go upon the deck, he passed through the memorable scenes of the Red Sea with cold indifference; did not care to recognize the historic towns and villages which, along its borders, raised their picturesque outlines against the sky; and betrayed no fear of the dangers of the Arabic Gulf, which the old historians always spoke of with horror, and upon which the ancient navigators never ventured without propitiating the gods by ample sacrifices.[2]

Even at the end of each stage of his journey he doesn't descend to earth, pointedly remaining in his cabin:

On this Friday, October 9th, he noted his arrival at Suez, and observed that he had as yet neither gained nor lost. He sat down quietly to breakfast in his cabin, never once thinking of inspecting the town, being one of those Englishmen who are wont to see foreign countries through the eyes of their domestics.[3]

And when his colleagues in London, discussing the possibility of finishing the course in the allocated time, say that if he wants to win the bet there will be absolutely no room for bad luck, Fogg is imperturbable, countering that he doesn't accept the notion of the unforeseen:

---

2. Ibid., 54.
3. Ibid., 44–45.

"Twenty thousand pounds!" cried Sullivan. "Twenty thousand pounds, which you would lose by a single accidental delay!"

"The unforeseen does not exist," quietly replied Phileas Fogg.

"But, Mr. Fogg, eighty days are only the estimate of the least possible time in which the journey can be made."

"A well-used minimum suffices for everything."

"But, in order not to exceed it, you must jump mathematically from the trains upon the steamers, and from the steamers upon the trains again."

"I will jump—mathematically."[4]

As the narrator later remarks, extending the mathematical metaphor, Fogg doesn't so much travel as revolve around the earth like an inanimate object:

Sir Francis Cromarty [had] made India his home, only paying brief visits to England at rare intervals; and was almost as familiar as a native with the customs, history, and character of India and its people. But Phileas Fogg, who was not travelling, but only describing a circumference, took no pains to inquire into these subjects; he was a solid body, traversing an orbit around the terrestrial globe, according to the laws of rational mechanics. He was at this moment calculating in his mind the number of hours spent since his departure

---

4. Ibid., 21.

from London, and, had it been in his nature to make a useless demonstration, would have rubbed his hands for satisfaction.[5]

Perhaps having reached the extremity of nontravel here, Fogg's goal is to remain for the shortest amount of time possible in each of the locations he passes through. Any visit might endanger his wager and the slightest delay would go against his temperament.

Obviously, the claim that he is traveling mathematically without stopping is constantly undermined throughout the novel, first of all because Fogg's final success can only be achieved thanks to the mathematical error of an extra day. In reality, Fogg has lost the bet as much as he has won it, and it would be just as valid to claim that he took eighty-one days to complete his journey.

But his failure is also due to the fact that Fogg—who attempts to become a pure machine as fits his natural predisposition—is constantly overtaken by subjectivity. Starting from the first moment he decides to make a digression in his journey, Fogg repeatedly fails to act like a machine and to effect a journey from which all subjectivity is banished.

The fact remains, though, that what we have here, at least in terms of its goal, is a serious attempt to travel while taking the fewest risks—an attempt that still gives him the opportunity to form an idea about the regions traversed, even if this high-speed locomotion does not protect Fogg from physical danger.

---

5. Ibid., 67

∼

If we take a closer look, crossing different regions of the world at top speed did not in any way prevent Phileas Fogg from gaining a fair impression of the places he refrained from visiting. When the occasion arose, he was even capable of demonstrating an encyclopedic knowledge of the local geography that he was happy to share with others—a knowledge gained without having traveled the slightest:

> Had he travelled? It was likely, for no one seemed to know the world more familiarly; there was no spot so secluded that he did not appear to have an intimate acquaintance with it. He often corrected, with a few clear words, the thousand conjectures advanced by members of the club as to lost and un-heard of travellers, pointing out the true probabilities and seeming as if gifted with a sort of second sight, so often did events justify his predictions. He must have travelled everywhere, at least in spirit.[6]

What's more, when he finds himself on the ground, so to speak, Fogg displays a fine appreciation of the context and the way one should behave in certain delicate situations. This is true of his passage through India,[7] during which he doesn't hesitate to make a detour to rescue a young Indian woman

---

6. Ibid., 3.
7. UP++

condemned by fanatics to die at the stake after her husband's disappearance.

> Mr. Fogg stopped him, and, turning to Sir Francis Cromarty, said, "Suppose we save this woman."
>
> "Save the woman, Mr. Fogg!"
>
> "I have yet twelve hours to spare; I can devote them to that."
>
> "Why, you are a man of heart!"
>
> "Sometimes," replied Phileas Fogg, quietly; "when I have the time."[8]

This quip about the amount of time he has should not obscure the fact that traversing the planet at great speed does not stop Fogg from preserving his critical faculties, those which strangers staying in a place and desirous of knowing, if not adopting, local customs might not. When faced with a concrete situation, he shows himself capable of responding to the problem posed by means of a universal judgement—something Kant in Königsberg would have been able to corroborate—which dictates his conduct.

It is remarkable that of all the people who witness the scene, including westerners, Fogg is the only one to display the obvious, humane reaction—to save the young woman's life. Fogg, who knows the country he is passing through only in theory—and perhaps precisely because his remote acquaintance allows him to keep a cool head—sees the situation outside of any cultural context.

---

8. Ibid., 88.

～

Might one risk a comparison and say that Phileas Fogg surveys countries like a hurried reader might survey a book? The notion of "surveying" a country actually leads us to wonder what similarities there might be between surveying a book and surveying a place.

The commonality of the term *to survey*, often used in both contexts, and the idea of rapidly crossing a space, should not be misleading, since the meaning of the verb differs substantially in each case.

The notion of surveying a book is often seen as deprecating and restrictive compared with the idea of a full, complete reading, which would do the text justice. It conjures up a fantasy of totality by implicitly opposing the idea of an integral reading that would follow the text from the first sentence to the last without leaving anything out.

The idea of surveying a place, on the other hand, has nothing deprecating about it. On the contrary, it suggests exploration, if not complete, at least attentive; traveling by foot rather than plane or train. In this sense, it would be more correct to say that Phileas Fogg traverses the regions on his itinerary than to say that he surveys them, since he concerns himself as little as possible with them, considering them obstacles that might only delay him.

This difference in meaning and denotation of the two kinds of surveying is related to the differences between the spaces involved. While both of the spaces are closed, the possibilities of surveying them differ fundamentally. It is possible to read a book in its entirety by following each line with your eyes, or possibly a finger, from the first to the last page. This doesn't necessarily mean that one would know it, or have understood it, or that one would remember it,[9] but in purely material terms, the process can be envisaged.

You might ask yourself what the equivalent of this integral reading might be in terms of a location, since a comparable route is lacking. In fact, there is no fixed route within space—networks and roads not being concordant—analogous to this network consisting of the lines of a text. If we think in terms of physical circulation, the logical question would be after how many kilometers—or, in terms of time, after how much time spent somewhere—could a traveler be considered to know a place, without forgetting that some people can spend their entire lives in the same place without really being able to say that they know it.

≈

Talking about a country or any other place always implies making a double selection. To start with, you must pick out from the vast array of possible images engendered by a place the ones you are going to focus on. However unlikely it is not to find any references to the Great Wall of China in his work, Marco Polo would be perfectly within his rights to argue to the skeptical reader that, given the immensity of the Chinese territory and what it offers to the visitor's curiosity, he was compelled to be selective.

---

9. See Pierre Bayard, *How to Talk About Books You Haven't Read* (New York: Bloomsbury, 2007).

This first selection process is linked to a second selection that is less obvious but just as essential. The choice of focusing on not so much a particular place, which wouldn't make much sense, but a particular image of a place means making sense of reality by cutting it up and organizing it. Choosing to describe a particular image from the vast array of possibilities offered by a space cannot be done without linking that space to a discourse that gives it meaning and integrates it into the greater unity of a reflection or vision.

This dual selection process leads to two different kinds of danger that few travelers manage to avoid. The first is the risk of getting lost in the details. Faced with the enormous diversity of possible routes and combinations—many more than one could physically fit into a book—there is a great danger of privileging to the point of blindness some randomly encountered secondary detail about the place traversed.

The second danger, in opposition to the first, is to get lost not in individual judgment but, on the contrary, in collective judgment—that is to say, only approaching unknown spaces by way of those preconceived opinions with which common places are constructed.[10] This is the kind of danger that Phileas Fogg seems to want to avoid when he refuses to play the tourist:

As for the wonders of Bombay—its famous city hall, its splendid library, its forts and docks, its bazaars, mosques,

---

10. See Bertrand Westphal's *La géocritique: Réel, fiction, espace* (Paris: Les Éditions de Minuit, 2007), 234, on stereotypes and ethnotypes attached to place.

synagogues, its Armenian churches, and the noble pagoda on Malabar Hill, with its two polygonal towers—he cared not a straw to see them. He would not deign to examine even the masterpieces of Elephanta, or the mysterious hypogea, concealed south-east from the docks, or those fine remains of Buddhist architecture, the Kanherian grottoes of the island of Salcette.[11]

What Fogg is wisely refusing here is the fact that however great the attraction of the sights proposed to him, they would mean following a preestablished route compiled by the general opinion of his predecessors, a route along which he would be as much at risk of missing the place by becoming absorbed in the community of opinions as of getting lost in infinite detail.

∼

The fact that we do not have to contend with hypothetical real places when traveling but with arbitrary, subjective images, taken from an infinite number of representations, only makes it more essential to seek out what I have called "a view of the whole" in connection with books.[12]

I had borrowed this notion of a view of the whole from Musil's *The Man Without Qualities*, where it is used by a librarian who takes care never to open a single book—he only allows himself to read catalogs—in order to keep a

---

11. Verne, 62.
12. See Bayard, *How to Talk About Books You Haven't Read*.

general perspective of his library and of all books in general. A general perspective doesn't consider each book separately but in its general relationship to other books and culture as a whole.

This "view of the whole" gives Phileas Fogg the appropriate means of traveling across many different countries at the greatest possible speed—the velocity being a token of the breadth of his vision—without dwelling in any particular place, nor focusing his attention on any secondary detail in each of them.

The point of maintaining a view of the whole is first of all to avoid getting lost in the details in which the traveler might drown at any point. Without the guide of the itinerary provided by the lines of a book, the surveyor of a place, especially a large one, runs the risk of getting lost in the abundance of possibilities, without having any way of synthesizing them.

But having a view of the whole can equally help you to avoid the stereotypes that erect a barrier to any real knowledge of the area traversed. The possibility offered by the rapid circulation of a place of perceiving it in all its diversity helps us to avoid hasty generalizations by revealing its complexity and those parts of it that cannot be synthesized.

Ultimately, the view of the whole is connected to the free-floating attention that Freud recommends to the psychoanalyst, aimed at enabling him to perceive, behind the conscious rational discourse, the main lines of the unconscious that organize the discourse and the behavior of the analysand without his knowledge.

～

There is, therefore, more common sense than you might think to Phileas Fogg's strategy of fast travel. It might allow some people to win their bets and avoid financial ruin, but it also prevents us from becoming bogged down in all the trivial details about the regions traveled through or stooping to the approximations of general opinion without losing interest in the country traversed nor the people living there.

The idea of staying in your cabin for the entire journey highlights the importance of the imagination and reflection in our approach to place. These are activities that Fogg is able to commit himself to completely vis-à-vis the places passed through, with all the more energy because he doesn't waste precious time visiting them.

3

Places Others Have Talked About

(in which Édouard Glissant discovers a clever way of
visiting Easter Island without leaving his armchair)

HAVING A LOT OF imagination and knowing not to waste
time stopping on your way are not the only attributes you
need to be able to talk about places you haven't been to. A
third attribute is often indispensable and complements the
first two since it ensures an accurate report: the presence of a
reliable informant at your side.

The informant's function is to serve as a relay between
the armchair traveler and the place he refrains from visiting.
She will be the one who takes the risks instead of the
nontraveler, adding the necessary ingredients to the latter's
account. This is why it is important to select with care and
chose someone the writer trusts, whether she lives in the
place itself or agrees to travel there. The writer must have
complete peace of mind about the information he receives.

∾

Most of the time, the role of the informant will be entrusted to remote witnesses, or even dead ones, and to the intermediate agency of historical or contemporary texts about the places you want to describe.

The role that narratives play in journeys has long been signaled,[1] and those who have studied this have been able to clearly demonstrate their importance in discovering unknown places, particularly foreign countries. Just as reading one book recalls other books—either those evoked by the writer or others that come naturally to mind—traveling often involves reading preliminary texts, in particular those dedicated to the place one wishes to discover.

If Marco Polo was able to write about China with such accuracy without leaving the Venetian lagoon, if Phileas Fogg could talk with such confidence about countries he'd never even set foot in, it is not only due to their imagination, but it is also because they were great readers, able to experience travel by proxy, constructing their own personal memories through other people's journeys.

These travel books don't just provide information essential to the discovery of places you are preparing to travel to either physically or in the imagination. We should be wary of seeing the "relation of resemblance" between places and books as a one-way street, as though books resemble the places they describe or recount without the opposite being true.

---

1. See Christine Montalbetti, *Le voyage, le monde et la bibliotheque* (Paris: Presses universitaires de France, 1997).

Inversely, places, by dint of being frequented by books and their readers, end up resembling them and adapt, with or without resistance, to the image given to them.[2] You might therefore be equally justified in starting, and even ending, your quest with books if you want to discover foreign places.

~

An essential support to the armchair traveler, the informant in writing is nevertheless somewhat inconvenient. Whatever the originality or liveliness of his account, he can hardly be questioned in greater depth. Solely relied upon, the testimony also lacks the vivacity of a firsthand retelling and the contributions such an account might make to becoming acquainted with places visited in the mind.

This is why an oral witness is the ideal informant: you can question him as you wish about what he has seen, it being possible to communicate verbally in order to perfect your knowledge, without having to go to the place for further investigation. But it is not that easy to find someone who has traveled to the place you wish to talk about and in particular, someone who has enough time to reply at length to a multitude of questions. And it is even more difficult, even if this is the ideal solution, to find someone in your own circle who is prepared to travel in your place.

One of the writers who successfully resolved the problem of the informant is Édouard Glissant. Having decided to visit

---

2. See Bertrand Westphal, *La géocritique*, 252.

Easter Island[3] in his old age and write a book about it but being too worn out to go himself, the only solution was to seek recourse to travel by proxy:

> Since it was impossible for me to go to the island in person, I found myself having to come to terms with the fate of those who can no longer spend an entire day on an airplane, just as it marks out for other places those people unable to hoist themselves up to snowy summits or venture across icy steppes or plunge into jungles.[4]

Unable to travel to Easter Island himself for health reasons, Édouard Glissant decided to send his wife, Sylvie Séma. Her mission was to travel in his place and furnish him with the information he needed to write about it:

> We agreed to work in tandem and to visit the island in two ways that might complement each other: Sylvie on the ground, as one might say (she would fly to Santiago, she absolutely wanted to carry on to Valparaiso, to this universal childhood dream, then she would continue to Easter Island, which meant twenty-four hours flying at least). And me, through the commentary I would give on what she sent to me and the things she brought back: notes, impressions, drawings, films and photos; and through the order or chaos of the literary nature she

---

3. DP++

4. Édouard Glissant (in collaboration with Sylvie Séma), *La terre magnétique. Les errances de Rapa Nui, l'île de Pâques* (Paris: Éditions du Seuil, 2007), 9. English translation by Michele Hutchison.

would help me bring to these documents and to her feelings grasped in this abrupt way.[5]

What's constructed in this way is an entity of two people, one of whom—rather pleasingly called "the female visitor"[6] in the book—visits the terrain in person and takes all the risks, while the other, remaining comfortably at home, gives his imagination free rein and engages himself in the labor of writing:

> The two of us, Sylvie and me, were like ethnographers of the encounter, one was the body working on the spot, the other the imagination, imbibing all of the physical space, walking down the valleys of generations and paddling up the brooks of genealogies, except that we were not troubled at all by descendants or heirs.[7]

This intelligent method, which allows for a separation of body and mind, has many advantages, including focusing all physical dangers on one person, the second member of the team being able to dedicate himself to the essential—an accurate perception of a place and its reconstruction in writing.

≈

If we examine resorting to travel by proxy in Édouard Glissant's case, it turns out to be quite complex because the

---

5. Ibid.
6. Ibid., 12.
7. Ibid., 34.

information the "visitor" gives to the writer is not uniform but falls within distinct categories. In fact, Glissant has carefully worked out an entire system to avoid traveling in which his wife is the key feature but not the only one.

This system requires, first of all, having access to external written sources, beginning with the abundance of literature inspired by the mythical island. Glissant refers to texts by Pablo Neruda, such as the poem "La Rosa separada," which is devoted to Easter Island, and of which he had a French translation.[8] But other less direct references, such as Herman Melville,[9] Alain Borer[10] or Alfred Métraux,[11] slip into the text at certain moments, informing it.

Furthermore, there were evidently a number of oral commentaries and diaries that are not directly shared with the reader but that are integral to the book since Glissant began writing using these firsthand testimonies provided by the person in whom he had placed his full confidence to help him provide a complete picture.

But Sylvie Séma also gave Glissant the drawings she made of the island and these accompany the text. They are abstract drawings—for example, of plants or trees—which don't claim to provide a realistic representation of the place but mark out particular unique details that struck the visitor and that she uses to try to enable her faraway companion to be present.

Finally, Sylvie Séma is equipped with a small camera, allowing her to regularly send pictures of the island to her

---

8. Ibid., 81.
9. Ibid., 13.
10. Ibid., 12.
11. Ibid., 47.

husband and bring certain secondary witnesses to his attention. This is the case with one of the local inhabitants called Betty whom she considers a prospective second informant, able to provide complementary information:

> Betty really wanted to speak to me, at least I thought so, through the miniscule camera that Sylvie had with her. She found it amusing to imagine me. She looked past the device, to where she might expect to find me, and where she guessed I'd be when I unrolled the film.[12]

This system of polyphonic transmission, when it can be perfected, comes close to the ideal solution because it offers the armchair traveler a whole sequence of information—all the richer for coming from multiple sources—and at the same time allows him to avoid the risks of actual travel and to conserve the benefits of a view of the whole.

Moreover, the barrier formed by the distance between the visitor and the armchair traveler is frequently crossed to the extent that the words of the witnesses interviewed blend in with Glissant's writing, as though he had actually met them, as though he had become familiar with them to the extent of them helping him to write the book, as though he had internalized them, so that by the end it is quite impossible to tell who is speaking.

In any case, you only need to open Glissant's book to see how efficient this system of delegation is. Even if he doesn't set foot on Easter Island, Glissant does not hesitate to provide

---

12. Ibid., 28.

lavish, sensitive descriptions, demonstrating the profound knowledge he has acquired of the place, undoubtedly much keener than the knowledge he would have obtained by staying on the island himself, even for a long period of time. This wouldn't have necessarily given him a view of the whole.

To give an idea of the power of the encounter, let us consider as an example this evocative description of the eucalyptuses on the island:

> The forest of eucalyptus trees: sentinels along the periphery of the Rano Raraku Volcano. One sees immediately that several trees with twisted branches are marked, you would use the word *chargé*—laden—in Antillean creole, or even *habités*—inhabited. They provide the only shade on the island. Their leaves make a tinny rustling sound when the winds descend onto the water of the crater in the evenings, producing crepuscular music.[13]

Or what about this portrayal of one of the island's volcanos, whose description draws on all of the traveler's senses and demonstrates the intensity of his presence in the place, as though simultaneously inscribed on different planes of perception:

> At the bottom of the volcano, the grasses and the rushes are cut up into bars rolling across the water, upon which the shadows of the sky and the moving colors of the rushes in turn inscribe the words carried by the winds

---

13. Ibid., 40.

of Asia and America, which mix with those from Micronesia or New Zealand, news of families that have grown up on Polynesia or on the Marquesas, which rebound onto a pyramid of stones like a marker, a sextant of heavens, earth and seas, or even to the center of the world. Everything is soft and one feels brushed by the light and the heat of the stones and the beating of the sea and the wind and the rain that is so light and the limpidity of the inhabitants' eyes, it is the opposite of aggression, of the violence of a place and its mythologies . . .[14]

In his search of a vision of the whole, Glissant does not only interest himself in natural features and landscapes but also in the inhabitants of the island, whose bodies, which he admires at length, prove fascinating in their massiveness:

Something that continues to amaze us, once we arrive on the island, is the flagrant massiveness of the bodies, a race of statues, masculine statures, mainly. Are the women and children kept apart for a reason unknown to us? Are they kept on a kind of adolescent diet?[15]

But, given that this is about a visit to Easter Island, a chapter on the statues is clearly expected from the writer, who acquits himself remarkably well of the given exercise, proving the wisdom of his decision to stay at home:

---

14. Ibid., 46.
15. Ibid., 16.

The island is a body which has seen the arrival of the material of all the other islands that preceded it; the island is growing as though to measure up to the bodies of the rows of statues, embedded in their space, it seems, midbelly, which become larger and larger as time passes, challenging artisans' techniques. These statues have brought together the imaginary worlds of statues and votive objects that preceded them on these island routes; it is the reason they seem so immense in size and in their wisdom: they are the repositories of the end of the road.[16]

∾

Having stayed on Easter Island myself, I can testify to the quality of Glissant's representations. In fact, he manages to resolve, with great poetic feeling, a whole series of problems with which a writer or painter is confronted when wishing to give an account of the island and its unusual atmosphere, represented with good reason in the legends it has given rise to since time immemorial.

How not to be struck, even if he was right not to leave out the eucalyptus forests where a few bears still roam, by the barren impression that emerges from these expanses without watercourses, without vegetation, as though abandoned by the gods and where the only trees still left alive resemble the mythical statues, some of which, unfinished, evoke the calcified trunks left behind by a great fire?

---

16. Ibid.

And how not to be impressed by the magic of its solemn volcanos and their interior lakes, starting with the largest on the island, the Maunga Terevaka, which seems to govern absolutely everything, keeping an eye on all goings on from its outcrop? And how not to bow down before Rano Raraku and the Rano Kau, whose geometric summits seen from afar resemble Aztec pyramids awaiting their sacrifices?

This savageness of the interior is complemented by that of the coasts, where waves of radiant blue, several meters in height, relentlessly beat against the black rocks of the shore as though they had decided to lay siege to the island until they manage, after eroding the foundations, to make it disappear.

As far as I can recall, the village of Hanga Roa is the only agglomeration on the island and the last human presence as far as the eye can see, offering to the visitor, with its few poorly stocked shops, its hotels and its isolated palm trees, a face a little more hospitable that contrasts, for the brief time taken to cross it, with the desolate brutality of the rest of the island.

∼

If using an informant allows you to gain an idea of places you do not visit, and if Glissant does not hesitate to describe an island he has never visited, we shouldn't forget that this type of relayed description is necessarily coupled with a loss of information:

> True ethnographers always have secret sources. We were the same, but we readily accepted it. Except that one of us had never even physically experienced this place,

aside from in his mind. It was enough for us, for example, and even if it was just by convention, to touch hands.[17]

But the loss of information experienced by the remote traveler, far from being a deficiency, is, on the contrary, perceived here by the writer as a positive factor that further justifies the choice of method:

> Through the double agency of Betty and the small camera, I inhabit this movement and this precariousness of elements. It is another way of benefiting from the attentions of the technique, even the most rudimentary kind, the grayish reproductions perhaps allowing me to guess at what perfect details the image would have revealed. It seems then that the magnetic resonance of the earth passes through the lack of definition of the small screen; Betty, calm and attentive enough to explain the most everyday things, suddenly deciphers something in this resonance and reads into this ephemerality; she becomes swathed in the unknown.[18]

If the informant provides indispensable information, she also constitutes an element of fuzziness and interference or jamming. Yet we might suppose that one of the interests of using her services is not just what she brings to the process but also what is lost, as though there were a real fecundity to this imprecise practice:

---

17. Ibid., 34.
18. Ibid., 30.

Betty took a scatty pleasure in mixing up the memories of the places she'd been to. She thought she was matching them up and that she had better arrange them all along her route as she went.[19]

Using the intermediary of another person is effectively giving oneself the means to take a detour though a different subjectivity, one that both enriches and distances. It is not only what the other person provides that counts, but also what she misses and, thanks to her participation, disperses, offering food for thought on the way.

Affording oneself another person's point of view means gaining an experience of a place different from what is traditionally associated with traveling—which aims, in a fantasy of omnipotence, in mastering the unknown—to wit an enriching experience that we might qualify as *nontravel*,[20] but whose heuristic value Glissant experiences thanks to his devoted companion.

∽

We are reminded again in Glissant's example just how fragile the division between travel and nontravel is. Although he stayed at home, Glissant still managed to give himself all the means to get to know Easter Island profoundly, means he

19. Ibid., 26.
20. Alain Roger already propounded this idea ("Barbarus hic ego" in *Ecrire le voyage*, Presses de la Sorbonne nouvelle, 1994) as did Thangam Ravindranathan (*La ou je ne suis pas*, Presses Universitaires de Vincennes, 2012) but in the sense of displacement.

wouldn't have had if he had patrolled it meter by meter. And, his wife's name being on the cover, ultimately the reader is dealing with a double author claiming to be the traveler.

When faced with such a complicated case, it becomes difficult to know whether Glissant did or didn't go to Easter Island. He would be perfectly entitled to say he knew the island, and perhaps even better than its inhabitants who have stayed too close to the object of perception to be able to talk about it with the necessary distance.

Places You've Forgotten

(in which we see, together with Chateaubriand,
that an island can move thousands of miles
between one text and another)

IF MARCO POLO'S TRAVEL narratives have long been considered reliable and of great scientific interest for the original information they offer on unknown parts, the same cannot be said of Chateaubriand, who has elicited great doubts among literary historians.

These doubts were so great that Chateaubriand quickly acquired a solid reputation as an armchair traveler once the veracity of his accounts had been investigated. Chateaubriand is more appreciated for the quality of his writing and the poetic force of his evocations than for the precision of his geography or the accuracy of his chronologies.

∼

Of all the journeys that Chateaubriand recounted in detail, two in particular caught the critics' attention. The first, the most famous, is a journey he made—that is to say, essentially didn't make—to North America[1] during the course of 1791, a journey he would expound on inexhaustibly and that he would keep returning to in his writing.

It is difficult to establish today with any accuracy the stages of Chateaubriand's voyage. It is assumed that he sailed from Saint-Malo on April 8, 1791, arriving in Baltimore on July 10. He then would have gone up the Hudson toward Niagara Falls, where, suffering from an arm injury, he apparently stayed for a month. But this episode itself isn't completely documented, and there is no certainty that Chateaubriand actually went as far as the falls, which were difficult to access at that time, braving hostile nature and its inhabitants to do so.

If he did reach them, the next step of his journey is not clear at all. Chateaubriand says that he left the region in early September, and having heard of Louis XVI's arrest in Vincennes, departed from America on December 10. It is improbable that he would have reached Pittsburgh so quickly and in particular the Mississippi River and the Floridas.[2] The descriptions he has left us of these regions, in particular in *Memoirs from Beyond the Tomb*, are therefore, in all probability, entirely fictitious.

In a well-researched article on the question of Chateaubriand's travels around America, Raymond

---

1. VP+

2. During Chateaubriand's time, the Floridas extended across a territory much larger than what is now called Florida and included a large area of the Southern States.

Lebègue,[3] in line with numerous critics including Sainte-Beuve, reaches the conclusion that all of the second part of the journey—in which one sees the writer go down to Ohio, discover the Mississippi, then visit the Floridas before going back up toward New York—a section remarkable as much for the quality of its descriptions as for the importance of its geographical information—can be classified as pure fiction.

He bases his argument on the strange composition of Chateaubriand's *Travels in America*, in which the writer skimps on details about the places he has seen, as well as the dates of his trip, preferring to increase the number of scientific observations and general political comments—and on the numerous contradictions between the different versions, as well as on the unlikelihood of the specifics.

The fact that he didn't go through the places he talks about did not at all prevent Chateaubriand, we imagine, from describing them with unfaltering confidence and great attention to detail, like in this passage about the Floridas:

We went fishing. The sun was about to set. In the foreground were sassafras, tulip trees, catalpas and oaks whose branches displayed skeins of white froth. In the middle ground, the most charming tree rose up, the papaya that one could have taken for a chiselled silver stylus mounted on a Corinthian urn. Balsams, magnolias and sweet gums dominated the background.

---

3. "Le problème du voyage de Chateaubriand en Amérique," *Journal des savants* I, no.I (1965), 456–65.

The sun set behind this curtain: a ray gliding across the dome of a grove sparkled like an emerald embedded in the dark foliage; the light diverging between the trunks and the branches projected rising columns and mobile arabesques onto the lawns. Above were lilacs, azaleas, vines girdled around gigantic bouquets; above clouds, some of them fixed promontories or old towers, others floating, tinted with rose or strung with silk.[4]

A similarly lively description animates this other passage, situated a little further along in the text, which one would consider accurately witnessed if the narrator hadn't slipped in for the attentive reader a discreet allusion to his memory problems:

Abandoned by my companions, I rested beside a cluster of trees: their shadows, glazed with light, formed the penumbra in which I was seated. Fireflies shone among the dark shrubs and were eclipsed when they passed through the moonbeams. The sound of the lake ebbing and flowing could be heard, the goldfish leaping, and the occasional cry of a diving bird. My gaze was fixed on the water; I gradually slid into that drowsiness familiar to those who travel the world's highways: I lost all clarity of recollection.[5]

---

4. François-René de Chateaubriand, *Mémoires d'outre-tombe* I [*Memoirs from Beyond the Tomb*], (Paris: Le Livre de poche, 2009), 515. English translation by Michele Hutchison.
5. Ibid., 516.

We should note that if we are to believe some of his biographers, not only did Chateaubriand not go to the places he described, but some of his most memorable encounters were also invented. This applies to his conversations with George Washington—which are probably fictional—and also his love affairs with two inhabitants of the Floridas, which were undoubtedly the fruit of his fertile imagination.

∾

Chateaubriand's second journey that provoked doubts was the one he made in 1806 to the Middle East and of which he gives a detailed account in *Itinerary from Paris to Jerusalem*.

Michel De Jaeghere dedicated an entire book, *Le menteur magnifique* (The magnificent liar), to the falsifications that Chateaubriand engaged in during the first part of his journey, his stay in Greece.[6] Retracing the writer's journey step by step and without holding his fabrications against him, given how much he admired his capacity to transform fragments of reality into literature, De Jaeghere studies in detail all of the liberties taken with the geographical truth.

Often they are a matter of simple exaggeration, like for example when Chateaubriand suggests that he was the first person to identify the ruins of Sparta, while everyone who lived in the Mistra region had known of its location for a long time. Or when, having arrived at the site, which consisted of just a few stones, he attempted to reconstitute the entire town in his mind.

---

6. VP-

At other moments, Chateaubriand deliberately changed the dates of his travels—this is the case for Athens, which he covers in a few days—in order to hide the fact that he did nothing more than have a quick glance at some of the major Hellenic sites, it being difficult in a serious travelogue to admit having neglected them.

At other times, such as for the south of the United States, Chateaubriand completely invents his sojourns or tours. This is especially the case with the descriptions he furnishes of Corinth, Megara and Eleusis, towns he could not have passed through if one pays attention to the dates given and recovered by various witnesses of his travels, ignoring his "fanciful chronology."[7]

As with his travels to the United States, not having visited a particular place does not prevent Chateaubriand from providing attentive and punctilious descriptions, like this masterful description he gives of the site at Corinth:

> Even from the foot of the Acrocorinth the view is enchanting. The villagers' houses, fairly large and well maintained, are spread out in clusters across the plain, among mulberry, orange and cypress trees; the vines, which provide the country with its wealth, give the countryside a fresh and fertile air. They are neither hung

---

7. Michel De Jaeghere, *Le menteur magnifique* (Paris: Les Belles Lettres, 2006), 227. "We should admit then that Fauvel wasn't wrong when he wrote that Chateaubriand arrived in Athens by sea. That he never set foot in Corinth, Megara and Eleusis. That he invented his visits, drawing inspiration from travelers who had preceded him in Attica" (239). English translation by Michele Hutchison.

in garlands on the trees as in Italy, nor trained low as around Paris. Each vine forms a bundle of isolated greenery from which the grapes hang like crystals in the autumn. The summits of Parnassus and Helicon, the Gulf of Lepan'to, which resembles a magnificent canal, and Mount Oneius, covered with myrtles, form the north and east horizon of the view, while the Acrocorinth and the mountains of Argolis and Sicyon rise to the south and west. As for the Corinthian monuments, they no longer exist.[8]

This is a highly attractive portrait of a place, even if fully appreciating its worth requires moving it several hundreds or thousands of years into the future, when time will have completed its work of destruction. Every visitor to Corinth, contrary to what Chateaubriand claims in his last sentence, is still able to admire its magnificent archaeological site today.

∾

If Chateaubriand can so readily allow himself to invent travel destinations without ever having visited them, it is because he bases his work, like his predecessors did, on a whole series of readings that structure his perception and his

---

8. François-René de Chateaubriand, *Itinéraire de Paris à Jérusalem et de Jérusalem à Paris* (Paris: Gallimard, Folio classique, 2005), 149. The strange claim that there aren't any ruins left at Corinth while it is impossible not to see them is one of the things that convinced critics that Chateaubriand never set foot there. English translation by Michele Hutchison.

imagination of space, readings that interpose themselves between the world and himself. His encounter with countries is fundamentally intertextual—that is to say, it is also an encounter with books, which are called to the rescue whenever he is forced to skip a step.[9]

The references mainly fall into three categories. First of all, there are the travelogues, responsible for providing the necessary components to his accounts of nontravel. Chateaubriand regularly leans on a whole series of testimonies left by authentic travelers who have ventured to the places he doesn't have time to visit. Thus he travels across Greece with authoritative texts at hand, referring to them either to better see the regions visited, or substituting a suitable book when he hasn't been to a particular place that he nevertheless feels compelled to describe.

Moreover, Chateaubriand likes to draw, explicitly or implicitly, from great classical or humanist texts that don't necessarily have a direct relationship with the places traversed but chime with the various thoughts running through his mind, allowing him to elevate his thinking. As Jean-Claude Berchet writes of his travels around Greece, "Certainly there isn't much to see in Sparta or Corinth or Salamis, but that's where Chateaubriand has appointments with Leonidas, Saint Paul, Themistocles."[10]

But there is a third scenario, a much more unusual one, in which Chateaubriand quotes his own texts. This phenomenon, more frequent in the trip to America than to

---

9. For more on the intertextuality of travel, see Bertrand Westphal, *Le géocritique*.
10. Ibid., 33.

the Middle East, relates to the fact that the writer revisits
the same journeys in several books set in different periods of
his life, leading him to quote himself, sometimes introducing appreciable variations.

   This self-referencing is of great interest to the reader
because it allows us to see the way in which, as time
progresses, concrete places, already rather manhandled
during their first appearance in his writing, are torn little by
little from their realistic context and made to obey literary
laws, indifferent to contingencies of place and time.

∾

These variations in the details are unimportant in
Chateaubriand's eyes. For him, intertextuality is linked to
the elevated viewing position that he adopts for all the
places he passes through, a position that approaches what I
defined earlier, quoting Musil, as a view of the whole.

   Avramiotti, who showed Chateaubriand around some of
the Greek sites, recounts one of their conversations as they
surveyed Argos:

> Visiting the citadel the next day, he told me that he had
> never enjoyed such a vast panorama as that offered by
> this hill. And I added that only captains taking the salute
> from their troops or painters drawing landscapes would
> be happy with this elevation and that a learned man
> would seek out each stone in his travels, each inscrip-
> tion, and take pleasure in comparing their authors with
> his personal observations. He replied that nature had

not made him fit for such servile studies and that all he needed was some height to immediately stir up pleasing images from fables and history from his memory. This response was precisely because, flying through the tree-tops of Olympus and Pindus, he placed towns, temples and buildings according to his whims.[11]

Trying his luck again, Avramiotti tries to convince Chateaubriand to give up his elevated position and venture out into the terrain, at least for a moment:

> I advised our traveler therefore to go and see the theater.
>   "I saw it as I arrived in Argos."
>   "Did you notice the seats carved into the rock, the Greek basic structure and the Roman superstructure?"
>   "I did not stray from my route to see such trifles; it suffices to have seen it in the distance."[12]

Commenting on the reactions of local guides to this refusal of "trifles," Jean-Claude Berchet notes in his preface to *Itinerary from Paris to Jerusalem*:

> For someone like Avramiotti or even Fauvel, Chateaubriand's visit would have been a small-scale event. Beforehand, they would have looked forward to showing off the splendors of their town to such an interesting guest, to demonstrating their own learning,

---

11. *Le menteur magnifique*, 39. Trans. Michele Hutchison.
12. Ibid., 40.

to showing him the discoveries they had made. But the visitor's mind was elsewhere. Contrary to the close-up view of these local specialists, he had always claimed the right to a faraway view, or rather a high-up view: a vision at once panoramic and personal.[13]

This idea of seeing things in their context or in a panoramic way, close to that of Phileas Fogg, is essential to Chateaubriand's conception of creation. He believes that he should not focus on details or geographical reality, but that his role is to research the things that might inscribe the place described in a larger dimension, the things that only literature allows us to access by its transformative force.

~

This manner of traveling will necessarily lead to memory problems when it comes to showing some precision after the fact. The example Chateaubriand sets with the divergent rewritings of his own travels perfectly illustrates the significance of forgetting when attempting to describe places, including those the narrator has actually been to.

This process of forgetting is all the more important in Chateaubriand's autobiographical writings because if the first versions of his trip to America are close enough in time to the trip itself, the account he gives in *Memoirs from Beyond the Tomb* comes several decades later and is therefore marked by the passage of time.

---

13. *Itinéraire de Paris à Jérusalem et de Jérusalem à Paris*, 14. Trans. Michele Hutchison.

The work of forgetting, if one can call it such, sometimes has extraordinary consequences, such as appreciable
differences in geography. This is true of an island that
Chateaubriand situates in Ohio in *Memoirs from Beyond the
Tomb*:

> We were driven along by a fresh breeze. The Ohio,
> swollen by a hundred rivers, sometimes got lost in lakes
> which opened up before us, at other times in forest.
> Islands rose up from the midst of the lakes. We sailed
> toward one of the largest, landing there at eight o'clock
> in the morning.[14]

The description of this island provides Chateaubriand
with the opportunity to include one of his precise, poetic
descriptions, the kind he is accustomed to, aimed at proving
his actual presence in the place:

> I crossed a prairie strewn with yellow-flowering
> ragwort, pink-plumed hollyhocks, and obolaria with
> purplish pappi.[15]

At the heart of this island is an Indian ruin, offering
the traveler a point of departure for one of his specialisms,
a meditation on vanished civilizations and the passage of
time:

---

14. *Mémoires d'outre-tombe*, 507. Trans. Michele Hutchison.
15. Ibid., 508.

An Indian ruin caught my attention. The contrast between this island and the youthfulness of nature, this human monument in a wilderness, caused a great torrent of emotion. Which people had lived on this island? Their name, race, the length of their stay? Had they existed while the world in whose breast they were hidden was ignored by three quarters of the planet? The silence of this people was perhaps contemporary to the clamor of great nations that have fallen silent in their turn.[16]

His prolonged visit to every nook and cranny of the island allows the poet, by elevating his thought to the heights of human history, to reflect on his own destiny:

A stream garlanded with Venus flytraps: a host of dragonflies buzzed around it. There were also humming-birds and butterflies that, in their most glittering baubles, jousted brilliantly with the iridescence of the flowers. In the midst of my wanderings and my studies, I was often struck by their futility. What? Could the Revolution, which weighed on me and which had driven me into the woods, inspire in me nothing more serious? What? During these days of upheaval in my home country, could I occupy myself with nothing more than descriptions of plants, butterflies and flowers? Human individuality serves to measure the smallness of the greatest of events.[17]

---

16. Ibid.
17. Ibid., 509.

The problem is that this island of such symbolic importance, meant to illustrate the fragility of mankind and the
impossibility of taking history's measure, has traveled quite a
lot itself. As Jean-Claude Berchet recalls, it was first situated
in what is now Florida at the time of *Travels in America*.[18]
Migrating, it then made a foray into the Mississippi at the
time of an 1834 manuscript, before, following its movement
northward, it found itself here in Ohio, several thousand
kilometers away, clearly justifying the epithet of "a floating
island."[19]

∼

As Jean-Claude Berchet, who describes *Memoirs from Beyond
the Tomb* as a "heteroclite manuscript,"[20] comments, it is
not that easy to reconstruct a journey several years after-
ward, and bad faith and poetic concerns are not necessarily
the only explanations one could put forward to explain
Chateaubriand's imprecision:

> The lengthy sequence that begins here and doesn't end
> until the beginning of chapter 5 is undoubtedly rooted
> in one or several actual experiences, but Chateaubriand
> struggles to localize them, or even differentiate them.

---

18. See Chateaubriand's *Études historiques* (Historical studies) and *Travels in
America*. The text is often close to that in the *Memoirs*, but the island is not in
the same place.
19. Ibid., 508, note.
20. Ibid., 507, note.

Let's not forget that, in reality, his 1791 journey had him cover enormous distances at the accelerated tempo he was so fond of, across regions that were still poorly signposted, poorly mapped . . . Furthermore, Chateaubriand soon added reading notes to his observations as a budding naturalist, as to the intense memories of certain scenes. The result was a heteroclite manuscript that knew many ups and downs and began to feed various fictions (*Atala, Les Natchez*). When for financial reasons Chateaubriand wrote the account of his travels to America thirty-five years later, and again when he gave the corresponding part of his *Memoirs* their final shape, these vast regions underwent a complete metamorphosis, which followed on from their initial lightning colonization. It became quite difficult in these circumstances to make old images that were strong but unanchored in any specific geographical space tally with the new realities of maps or scientific memoirs from 1832.[21]

This matter of forgetting leads us to ask ourselves if the border between travel and nontravel is not even more difficult to define than previously thought. A place we have forgotten, but which we did actually visit—when every trace of the trip has vanished from our memory, would that still count as a place traveled through?

In considering himself incapable of remembering whether he visited a particular place, Chateaubriand shows how the

---

21. Ibid.

question of knowing where one has been doesn't only give rise to answers that are positive or negative but also on occasion to intermediate responses often much more complex, reflecting the effects of time and the unreliability of memory.

And this is all the more so because Chateaubriand's particularity is not only to forget the places he has been to—all travelers go through that—but his ability to play on the creative, fecund character of forgetting, the kind of forgetting that accompanies every attempt to write one's own life story. Describing settling into the Valley of the Wolves in his *Memoirs*, he writes:

> I worked with delight on my *Memoirs*, and *The Martyrs* advanced; I'd already read several books to Mr. de Fontanes. I had installed myself in the midst of my recollections as in a large library: I consulted one then another, then I closed the register with a sigh because I noticed that the light destroyed the mystery as it entered. Light up the days of a life, and they will no longer be what they are.[22]

But, although it has negative consequences, this forgetting also opens up the path to fiction. In an 1844 letter to a

---

22. *Mémoires d'outre-tombe II*, quoted by De Jaeghere (op. cit. 279) in *Le menteur magnifique*, who comments on the passage: "The whole secret of the composition of *Itinerary* is perhaps summarized here: confusing books with memories, consulting memories without feeling obliged to follow them to the letter, the vague feeling that the truth loses something when bathed in light, that it should remain veiled to deliver its mystery." Trans. Michele Hutchison.

Canadian priest, Chateaubriand acknowledges his difficulty in separating real memories from fictitious ones:

> I mixed many fictions with real things and unfortunately the fictions gain a real character as time passes, which metamorphoses them.[23]

From this perspective, forgetting is not a deficiency but an essential element in the creative process. The "strong images" that Chateaubriand is interested in are not attached to an identifiable place or moment, even if a place and a moment are situated at their origin. They belong to an abstract space-time continuum, the spatial impression being coupled with a temporal impression, and searching for this justifies the traveler's no longer being able to precisely identify the conditions of emergence.

Following on from Glissant and others, Chateaubriand shows that a form of nontravel is necessary to the perception of place and to travel writing. Abandoning a perfect command of things, far from misleading the narrative, is more likely, by passing through the inner self, to do justice to unknown places by highlighting their universal appeal over their factual reality.

∾

These few examples of nontravel in no way exhaust the possibilities available to anyone averse to traveling for

---

23. *Mémoires d'outre-tombe*, 507, note. Trans. Michele Hutchison.

getting to know and to appreciate new places without leaving home, all the more so because the categories they illustrate are not mutually exclusive.

This means that the moment has arrived for a concrete study of a certain number of discourse situations in which we might be forced to talk about places we have not visited. Contrary to what one might think, the frequency of these situations is not negligible. But they are very complex and deserve to be studied with rigor if one wishes to try to find a reasonable solution to the delicate problems they pose the armchair traveler.

Talking About Travel

5

In the Field of Anthropology

(in which one discovers certain truths about
the morals of young Samoans thanks to
Margaret Mead)

IF THERE IS ONE field where the necessity of traveling is not
disputable, it is anthropology. While Lévi-Strauss may open his
most famous book, *Tristes tropiques*, with a provocative statement ("I hate traveling and travelers"), he then launches into a
detailed account of his own trips to Latin America, making it
clear that travel is crucial to the work of anthropologists and
that the profession would be impossible without it.

The sentiment that it is necessary is thus established as
something evidential in the common awareness. If you want
to analyze the behavior of foreign peoples, in particular
peoples living in distant lands, you must go to their home-
land and stay there for as long as possible in order to properly observe them and identify irrefutable scientific laws
based on firsthand observation.

∾

And what would we know today about not just the Samoan Islands[1] and the sex lives of their inhabitants but also about human sexuality without the efforts of Margaret Mead, without the journeys in search of other peoples she agreed to make in the 1920s for the benefits of science?

If her description of the Samoan Islands and the morals of its inhabitants is far from limited to portraits of sexuality, which in fact occupy only a few chapters, it is indisputably this part of her research that attracted readers' attention and contributed to the book's fame. The book, *Coming of Age in Samoa*, has become one of the classics of anthropology.

The central thesis of the work and the thing that assured its worldwide success is that Samoan sexuality is much more free than Western sexuality, and, in particular, that of North Americans, constrained as they are in their behavior by internalized taboos. The young Samoans are not afraid to have multiple experiences before marriage for the sake of experiment:

> The fact that educating one sex [the male sex] in detail and merely fortifying the other sex with enough knowledge and familiarity with sex to prevent shock produces normal sex adjustments is due to the free experimentation which is permitted and the rarity with which both lovers are amateurs ... Familiarity with sex, and the recognition of a need of a technique to deal with sex as

---

1. DP+

an art, have produced a scheme of personal relations in which there are no neurotic pictures, no frigidity, no impotence, except as the temporary result of severe illness . . .[2]

The most common way for two single people to have an affair is to meet in secret, this being also referred to locally as "under the palm trees":

> These clandestine lovers make their rendezvous on the outskirts of the village. "Under the palm trees" is the conventionalised designation of this type of intrigue. Very often three or four couples will have a common rendezvous, when either the boys or the girls are relatives who are friends. Should the girl ever grow faint or dizzy, it is the boy's part to climb the nearest palm and fetch down a fresh cocoanut to pour on her face in lieu of *eau de cologne*.[3]

But this general moral freedom also gives rise to other kinds of relationships between singles, such as public courting,[4] kidnapping (*avaga*) reserved for girls of higher rank,[5] or secret rape (*moetotolo*), where a man appropriates the favors destined for another by taking advantage of the cover of darkness:

---

2. Margaret Mead, *Coming of Age in Samoa* (New York: William Morrow & Company, 1928), 150–51.

3. Ibid., 92.

4. Ibid., 96–97.

5. Ibid., 104.

The need for guarding against discovery makes conversation impossible, and the sleep crawler [*moetotolo*] relies upon the girl's expecting a lover or the chance that she will indiscriminately accept any comer. If the girl suspects and resents him, she raises a great outcry and the whole household gives chase . . . The *moetotolo* problem is complicated by the possibility that a boy of the household may be the offender and may take refuge in the hue and cry following the discovery. It also provides the girl with an excellent alibi, since she has only to call out "*moetotolo*" in case her lover is discovered.[6]

Through these juicy anecdotes, Margaret Mead describes an idyllic society where the absence of major conflict and feelings of guilt as well as significant sexual freedom leads to a balanced adolescence without problems:

With the exception of the few cases to be discussed in the next chapter, adolescence represented no period of crisis or stress, but was instead an orderly developing of a set of slowly maturing interests and activities. The girls' minds were perplexed by no conflicts, troubled by no philosophical queries, beset by no remote ambitions. To live as a girl with many lovers as long as possible and then to marry in one's own village, near one's own relatives and to have many children, these were uniform and satisfying ambitions.[7]

---

6. Ibid., 93–94.
7. Ibid., 157.

It is a society that contrasts in its freedom and casual attitude with our Western way of life led in the clutches of multiple taboos, to which the Samoans' joie de vivre and their absence of complexes holds up a mirror:

> A boy declares that he will die if a girl refuses him her favours, but the Samoans laugh at stories of romantic love, scoff at fidelity to a long absent wife or mistress, believe explicitly that one love will quickly cure another ... Romantic love as it occurs in our civilisation, inextricably bound up with ideas of monogamy, exclusiveness, jealousy and undeviating fidelity does not occur in Samoa. Our attitude is a compound, the final result of many converging lines of development in Western civilisation, of the institution of monogamy, of the ideas of the age of chivalry, of the ethics of Christianity.[8]

∼

It is difficult today to understand the enormous readership there was for Margaret Mead's book in her time. The reason is that, independent of its enjoyable anecdotes about the sex lives of young Samoans, it formed part of a fundamental debate in American society in which it was a showpiece.

This debate revolved around the question of the extent to which the culture in which an individual grows up influences their behavior and the extent to which acquired traits

---

8. Ibid., 104–5.

due to this environment are more important than innate characteristics that would have determined their development in any setting.

For the cultural relativist movement, exemplified by anthropologists such as Ruth Benedict and Ralph Linton and to which Margaret Mead was connected, culture is a · determining factor in the establishment of personality and plays a more important role in its development than natural temperament produced by inherited traits.

But a statement like this is difficult to prove, given the great amount of interaction between peoples, which distorts the analysis. By becoming interested in a largely autonomous culture that she had not grown up in and that was different from Western culture, Margaret Mead was able to make significant advances for the cultural relativist theory.

She showed, in fact, with supporting evidence, that the guilt that weighs on sexuality in American society is by no means a foregone conclusion, and that a society like that of the Samoans, with its different morals, can lead to an uninhibited relationship with the body, allowing the young Samoans to experience sexual freedom under the palm trees.

∼

The debate around Margaret Mead's theories underwent a radical new turn when anthropologist Derek Freeman's 1983 work *Margaret Mead and Samoa: The Making and Unmaking of an Anthropological Myth* appeared. In this polemical book, the Samoan Island specialist explained that too much time had been spent thinking about the interpretation of the phenomena described by Margaret Mead without anyone taking the time to verify their actual existence beforehand, and that the purported sexual freedom of the young Samoans, which had fed imaginations across the globe, was a myth.

According to Freeman, Margaret Mead was well intentioned when she wrote her book, but she let herself become caught in a triple snare. The first trap was of the theoretical kind. The young anthropologist arrived in Samoa with the task of demonstrating the cultural relativist theory that was then fashionable in the United States and supported by her thesis adviser, Franz Boas. By showing that a society structured differently than the American model led to an authentic kind of sexuality, Margaret Mead significantly advanced the theory of cultural relativism. But, according to Freeman, she had cherry-picked the facts without realizing it and bent them to fit the theory she was trying to defend.

The second trap was a practical one. After having stayed in a Samoan village for ten days, Margaret Mead decided for reasons of personal comfort to move in with an American family that lived nearby. But in doing this she deprived herself of the opportunity of directly observing things that would have allowed her to verify her theories. Her poor knowledge of the Samoan language, whose basics she picked up while there, increased the distance between herself and the subjects she wished to study.

The third trap was intimately linked to the second one. At a remove from her field of observation, Margaret Mead was forced to rely on the testimonies of young female informants who came to visit her on a daily basis. According to Freeman, these women had the time of their lives with her. Faced with a young woman not much older than themselves, they let their imaginations run wild and invented a world of unbridled morals for her, with all the more liberating enjoyment since they actually lived in a universe with particularly oppressive morals:

> And when she persisted in this unprecedented probing of a highly embarrassing topic, it is likely that these girls resorted, as Gerber's Samoan informants have averred . . . [to] regaling their inquisitor with counterfeit tales of casual love under the palm trees.[9]

This is how the decision to describe a place from a distance by privileging the accounts of informants over personal observation led Margaret Mead to unwittingly construct a true fiction, later adopted without verification by generations of readers and scientists, who spent a lot of time trying to find convincing interpretations to account for nonexistent phenomena.

~

What Margaret Meads constructs from her trip to the Samoan Islands—at least if we are to follow Freeman's

---

9. Derek Freeman, *Margaret Mead and Samoa: The Making and Unmaking of an Anthropological Myth* (London: Pelican Books, 1994), 290

critical reading of it—could be called an *imaginary realm*, the expression having a double meaning.

It is an "imaginary realm" in the first instance, to the extent that the anthropologist's imagination, together with that of her informants, projects onto reality a series of fantasies which are both collective and individual. In this sense, the imaginary realm that Margaret Mead describes is set against the "real realm" or place, without this being in any way accessible—contrary to what Derek Freeman, whose own work has also been subject to criticism, believes.[10]

But "imaginary realm" can also be understood in a different sense, the one that J. M. Barrie, the author of *Peter Pan*, gives it when he invents an island where everything is perfect—his Neverland, accessed only by dreaming or flying. It is a melancholic projection of that childhood dominion from which every person has been expelled at a certain point in their lives, to their great distress. This place is all the more idealized because, never having existed, it cannot be found.

As they are in Margaret Mead and her female informants' fantasy, the Samoan Islands, where a happy rather than conflicted sexuality reigns and where the entire population makes love freely, are related to the island Peter Pan sought refuge on to avoid growing up. They embody the allegory of lost childhood, miraculously protected from the violence of the adult world.

---

10. For an overview of this controversy see Martin Orans, *Not Even Wrong: Margaret Mead, Derek Freeman, and the Samoans* (Novato, CA: Chandler & Sharp Publications in Anthropology and Related Fields, 1996).

It is understandable that this representation of the Samoans was met with such success in the world, because it corresponds to the general expectation that unknown travel destinations bring back to life the fantasy place where we once knew happiness and which we have been separated from for much too long. Whether it is correct or not, it has the merit of reminding us that it is difficult to access a place without immediately projecting onto it a grid of personal fantasies, impregnated with the obsessive dream of happy sexuality.

∽

But should this superiority that Margaret Mead accorded to an imaginary realm that piqued the world's imagination be condemned? Underlying the debate between Margaret Mead and Derek Freeman is one of the most fundamental notions in anthropology and sociology—*participant observation.*

The idea was born in the 1930s in the United States and defended in particular by sociologists from the Chicago school or authors close to this movement like William Foote Whyte. It met with immense success in several humanities disciplines where it opened the door to research and became the sine qua non of scientific activity.

For theorists of participant observation, the scientist should not just approach the subject of his study but merge with it for at least some time by participating in the same activities. It is not enough to observe, even from close up; you must place yourself in the same conditions or it will not be possible to feel what the subject or group you want to describe is experiencing.

True to this idea of participant observation, we see sociologists getting themselves hired by companies, participating in street protests, mixing with gangs of delinquents—all of the persuasion that physical proximity with their subject of study will enable them to report on it. In opposition to this, the theory of a view of the whole that I am developing in this book advocates the intellectual benefits of distance.

Driven by this idea borrowed from sociology, anthropologists have gone to live in the bosom of populations whose habits they have decided to study; they have shared their lives in the total conviction that by merging with the object of their study, they will be better able to give a faithful account of it.

∾

It is hard to quantify the devastation that the notion of participant observation has been allowed to wreak upon the scientific domain. The notion itself is based on a triple aberration that this book means to denounce.

The first of these aberrations is the naive idea that one has to be on the spot to be able to see and understand. Apart from the fact that being present physically is impossible in most cases (how should one report on the Battle of Waterloo?), it is obviously with the eyes of the mind that one must see, not those of the body, and if a physical presence is by no means pointless, it isn't the most important element in comprehending something, nor even in observing it.

The second aberration is the ignorance of the way in

which the presence of the subject in its field of research radically modifies it. Georges Perec in *Life: A User's Manual* evokes an anthropologist who tracks the Kubus tribe and wonders why they keep moving on mysteriously, before realizing that they are motivated by his own presence and that the tribe is trying to escape him above all else.

The third aberration is the ignorance of the heuristic power of both the imagination and of writing, two major components of knowledge that Marco Polo and Chateaubriand, among many others, have luckily drawn our attention to by relativizing the benefits of personal travel.

And neither should one underestimate the benefits that the anthropological fable elaborated by Margaret Mead and her brazen informants have contributed to our knowledge. Her book about the morals of the Samoans has done much to open up the debate about the education of adolescents in the United States and other countries by means of an imaginative but fertile example showing that it had harmful effects. As such, her Samoan novel was a useful fiction.

But above all, even supposing, as Derek Freeman does, that she was duped by her informants, Margaret Mead was able to capture a certain truth about their discourse and their history between the lines. Just as a fantasy is considered a form of truth about the subject in psychoanalysis, the fantasies that she gave form to in the company of young friends did have a real consistency, which, to her credit, she listened to.

∾

To combat the devastation wrought by participant observation, this book aims to defend what I propose to call *distanced observation*, as practiced by Marco Polo and Phileas Fogg.

The position that Margaret Mead, seated on her veranda at a good distance from the Samoan village, took has more than one thing in common with Marco Polo's at his Venetian retreat or Phileas Fogg's in his ship's cabin. By remaining at a certain distance from the subjects they wanted to write about and understand, both managed to capture profound truths, which they certainly wouldn't have been able to do if they'd obstinately kept their noses stuck in the objects of their study.

6

In the Media

(in which we wonder, in connection with
Jayson Blair, whether it is legitimate to
move tobacco fields in a newspaper article
or not)

A PROFESSION RATHER LIKE that of the anthropologist and
one with which it shares several points in common, journalism requires frequent travel, often abroad. As such, it is
considered dangerous, and the attempt to offer reliable
information to their readers costs countless journalists their
lives each year.

At this point, the obvious question is whether it might
not be more prudent to resort to observation from a distance,
like Marco Polo and Édouard Glissant did. This had the
double advantage of keeping them safe physically and
placing them in the privileged position of being able to
maintain a view of the whole, thus preserving the facts and
taking care not to get too involved.

∽

New York Times journalist Jayson Blair found himself in a difficult situation in late April 2003, a situation he describes at the beginning of his autobiography *Burning Down My Masters' House.*

He was invited to a meeting organized by some of his colleagues who wanted to talk to him about a recent article he'd published in the *New York Times* that showed some strange similarities to another article published not long before that in the *San Antonio Express-News.*

The article in question was about the family of a twenty-four-year-old soldier who had gone missing in Iraq, Sergeant Edward Anguiano, whom the journalist claimed to have interviewed at home in the town of Los Fresnos[1] near the Mexican border. The article didn't go unnoticed—it was featured on the front page of the *New York Times*, the dream of every journalist at the biggest daily paper in the world.

To defend himself against charges of plagiarism, Jayson Blair explained to his colleagues how, when he was researching the story, he put together a case file on his computer in which he saved all the documentation he had found on this family, including the article in the *San Antonio Express-News.* He told how, when he was writing his own text, he'd mixed up entire paragraphs of the article with his own notes without realizing it.

At the same time as he is giving an entirely satisfactory explanation, which seems to convince his colleagues, who are

---

1. DP-

used to this kind of mistake, Jayson Blair is aware that he isn't going to be able to maintain the illusion for that long. His lies are on a different scale from a simple error in managing information on his computer:

> The only problem, of course, was that it hadn't happened that way at all. I was the only one in the room who knew that I had never flown to San Antonio, had never rented a car at the small rental place across from the airport, and had never slept in it. I had never driven south down U.S. 77 in the blazing heat, had never taken a left onto Texas 100, never turned onto Buena Vista Drive, and never crossed the railroad tracks near the Anguiano household. I had never seen the Martha Stewart furniture on the patio, nor the shrine to Edward in one of the daughter's rooms. I had never missed my exit along the way, nor stopped in Brownsville, nor had I gone to the small town called Port Isabel along an inlet to the Gulf of Mexico. The truth was I had never left my apartment in Park Slope, Brooklyn.[2]

Finding himself increasingly cornered by his colleagues who, as the days passed, pressed him with questions, asked him to send them the pieces that could have caused the confusion between the two articles and investigated the expenses he'd claimed after his supposed trip to Los Fresnos,

---

2. Jayson Blair, *Burning Down My Masters' House* (New York: New Millennium Press, 2004), 5.

Jayson Blair finally decided to resign from the *New York Times* and enroll for treatment in a mental health clinic.

∾

It wasn't the first time that Jayson Blair had described places in his articles that he had never been to. The book he dedicated to his adventures is an attempt to explain to others, and also to himself, how, little by little, the technique of observation from a distance turned into a habit, if not a philosophy.

Writing articles from a distance wasn't something that happened to him suddenly but something that developed in reaction to a combination of circumstances. Blair started making minor breaches in journalistic etiquette, motivated by fatigue, recklessness and practical issues that occasionally prevented him from traveling, but without in any way turning this into a deliberate line of conduct.

When, due to ordinary forgetfulness, he is unable to attend a concert his newspaper has scheduled him to cover, he finds himself, ironically, very close to the place he is supposed to describe, without being able to enter it:

> Unfortunately, the one [article] that got the most attention was a story I wrote drunk and high. I was supposed to attend a concert benefit at Madison Square Garden late one Saturday night. I had every intention of going, but somehow found myself at a party at an assistant foreign editor's house on the Upper West Side. After a couple of drinks, I headed downtown to go to the Garden, but realized I did not have the proper credentials

to get in. So, instead, I headed to West Forty-third Street, where I watched the event on television, taking occasional breaks to go into the stairwell near the Continuous News Desk to snort a little cocaine off a cigarette box I would place on the railings.

Writing off of television was not that odd an occurrence at *The Times*. Mayoral news events and other stories were often handled that way by editors and reporters who would tune into New York 1 or C-SPAN coverage. It was just strange to do it when you were less than ten blocks from an event and had time to go report and then return and file.[3]

But, because of his negligence, problems of a practical nature multiply as time passes. One day, having missed the train, he doesn't have time to meet a professor he is supposed to interview and makes do with a telephone conversation.[4] Another time, when one of the paper's bosses calls him and asks where he is, he replies that he's in Norfolk while he's actually in the kitchen of his apartment, then he later calls him back from "Gaithersburg"—that's to say, his kitchen—the place his manager has sent him to in the meantime.[5] On a different occasion, he doesn't go to Maryland, though he does send in a local reportage piece as requested:

The story was, indeed, a fabrication, but it was so in the sense that I had not actually traveled to Hunt Valley,

3. Ibid., 198.
4. Ibid., 328.
5. Ibid., 354.

Maryland. I had cobbled together all of the details from my telephone conversations with Martha Gardner, and double-checked the descriptions with the photos that were filed by the photographer who had actually visited the house.[6]

As his illness gained ground and he began to feel more and more uncomfortable at the paper, Blair grew accustomed to never leaving his apartment and to systematically composing his articles from a distance, getting caught up in lies that, ultimately, he could not escape:

It was not until December 31 that it sunk in how bizarre my existence had become. I had not left the apartment in three days. I had all I needed in the ample supply of coffee that was helping me stay up. I only spent several hours each night sleeping. I was supposed to be in Lexington, Virginia, but I had isolated myself entirely. Even Zuza and her roommates believed that I was on the road. I even missed out on the New Year's Eve celebrations, when theoretically I could have been back, because I was cooped up in my apartment. I was beginning, once again, though this time without drugs, to have a secret life of my own, one that involved being locked up in a Brooklyn apartment, an obsessive and isolated world I was keeping secret from Zuza.[7]

---

6. Ibid., 286.
7. Ibid., 265.

~

Three explanations for this behavior, among many others, emerge from Jayson Blair's autobiography, allowing us to understand how he got himself into this paradoxical situation. The first is his psychological state, which he describes as manic-depressive, which leads him to go through phases of excitement and melancholy. He will seek treatment for this bipolar condition when he signs into a clinic after resigning from the *New York Times*.

The second explanation is his addiction to alcohol and drugs, which becomes worse, like that of many of his colleagues at the paper. The addiction helps him to curb his anxiety and to stand up to the demands of his employer and all the stressful periods he has to get through.

Finally, Blair feels, for ideological reasons, more and more uncomfortable at the *New York Times*, notably because of a number of editorial decisions that often seem to him to privilege those who report on sensational events liable to increase the paper's readership over articles of substance.

It is clear there is a pathological dimension to Jayson Blair's behavior, especially considering there was no way he could fail to be unmasked since he was writing for a paper whose audience was such that it would be impossible for his plagiarisms to go unnoticed for long.

However, even if Blair's breaches of journalistic ethics were inextricably linked to psychological problems, it is interesting to note that he did not believe they affected his work. On the contrary, he believed they allowed him to attain a higher degree of consciousness and to write better than he would have in a normal state:

> I cannot speak for the broader population, people at large or even generalize about a group of people. I can answer the question for me, and it is simply that at this fully psychotic stage, I was performing some of my best, although most fraudulent, writing.[8]

For this reason, if Blair developed intense feelings of guilt after his resignation, it is not certain, upon reflection, that they were entirely justified and that the criticisms made of this armchair traveler weren't exaggerated, especially if we decide to take the matter with a dose of philosophical salt.

∾

It is hard to deny, independent of any inquiry into journalistic ethics, that Jayson Blair's apparent flippancy was in reality accompanied by authentic documentary research and a real concern for accuracy.

Jayson Blair paid attention to detail—as much to the places, as the buildings, as the people—when writing the article that caused his downfall, and the account he gave of his time in the town of Los Fresnos included great meticulousness, even if it was made up:

---

8. Ibid., 287.

I lied about a plane flight I never took, about sleeping in a car I never rented, about a landmark on a highway I had never been on. I lied about a guy who helped me at a gas station that I found on the Internet and about crossing railroad tracks I only knew existed because of aerial photographs in my private collection. I lied about a house I had never been to, about decorations and furniture in a living room I had only seen in photographs in an electronic archive maintained by *Times* photo editors.[9]

He didn't hesitate to provide this information, expanding on the details, as he attempted to reassure one of his colleagues who had expressed doubts about his presence in Los Fresnos:

"Listen, Jim, I was there. I remember the beads that hang in the archway between the kitchen and a room where a shrine is. I remember the pictures in one of the daughter's rooms. I remember the back door of the kitchen leading to the patio. I remember the furniture. I remember that there was a satellite dish on the front lawn, an American flag and I think a POW or MIA flag also. I remember a tree on the left side of the house. I remember a truck being parked in the driveway. I remember the plants on the front of the house. I remember a ton of details."

"Okay, okay," he said.[10]

---

9. Ibid., 1.
10. Ibid., 17.

Now, it is important to note that in his articles, Blair didn't just reel off a load of nonsense, but taking care to be accurate, even from a distance, he went to the trouble of sourcing information each time, both by telephoning the people concerned and by gathering as much documentation as he could on the topic at hand.

Sometimes he even added details when they seemed necessary to bolster the impression of authenticity. So when he specifies certain details to convince his colleagues that he did go to Los Fresnos, they are an extension of the things that featured in the article itself, dated April 26, 2003, where the reader is treated to a thorough description of the patio where the missing soldier's mother, Juanita Anguiano, is standing.[11]

And in another of his articles that was equally criticized, dating this time to March 27, 2003, his taste for detail was such that the father of another missing soldier, a resident of Virginia, Gregory Lynch, was surprised to learn when reading the *New York Times* that his house looked out over tobacco fields and pastures, something he'd never noticed before.[12]

This proliferation of plagiarized or completely made-up details might seem questionable in itself. It might also have to do with the fact that Blair had a different logic from that of his confreres and that he was keen to give the reader—at the risk of placing tobacco fields beneath the windows of one of his interviewees if he deems it necessary—a particular

---

11. "Aftereffects: The Missing; Family Waits, Now Alone, for a Missing Soldier," *New York Times*, April 26, 2003.

12. "A Nation at War: Military Families; Relatives of Missing Soldiers Dread Hearing Worse News," *New York Times*, March 27, 2003.

impression, one that takes precedence over geographical correctness.

~

If we leave aside the moral dimension of journalistic trickery, Jayson Blair's story does pose the almost philosophical question, already latent in our previous examples, of knowing what it actually means *to be in a place*.

Every experience of writing can tell us something the many followers of religions know, namely that physical presence is only one of the possible modes of presence and not necessarily the most profound. The resolute struggle of armchair travelers against the ravages of participatory observation, whether theorized or not, plays out at this point.

In many scenarios in private or public life, *psychological presence* should not be confused with *physical presence*. First, the latter is no guarantee of anything at all. I could very well be physically present during a conversation, like a student not listening in class, and find myself in reality somewhere else, in a completely different scenario, having voluntarily absented or exiled myself.

Conversely, there are many ways of being present to another and to the world that don't in any way imply physical presence. In romantic life, in religious life, just as in scientific research, artistic life and history writing, many forms of presence to another or at an event can be identified that don't necessitate physically being there.

In the area of our psychological lives, such as it is reconstructed by psychoanalysis, physical presence is not that important where psychological reality is concerned. People who are absent, as well as people who have died, can play a decisive role in our lives; they can even be experienced as more present than the living—since they are indeed present.

Naturally, the evaluation of journalistic activity cannot embrace these kinds of considerations, and we can't blame Jayson Blair's colleagues for pushing him toward the door. The fact remains, though, that the power of his articles poses questions about the notion of presence that it is impossible to dismiss with a wave of the hand.

~

In fact, in his repeated practice of armchair travel, Jayson Blair undoubtedly violates the elementary rules of journalism, while at the same time acting like a real writer.

It is noteworthy that the question of knowing whether Blair physically went to Los Fresnos or not, which obsessed his colleagues, completely eclipses a different question that is not unimportant and that interests every writer, namely to what extent did the account of his visit allow the newspaper's readers to understand the painful experiences of the families of soldiers sent to Iraq?

As it happens, understanding and writing about this experience consists of real work that cannot be confused with the fact of physically visiting or not visiting the place where the families lived. We are talking here about psychological presence, and this has nothing to do with traveling, even if it is conceivable that in certain cases, travel might help in understanding the suffering of the people involved.

There are two different kinds of truth at play in journalism on the one hand and in writing on the other; one is strictly referential, the other is not. Journalistic truth, the thing by which Jayson Blair was judged, looks to bring together language and the world and as such requires accurate descriptions. It therefore cannot accept the fact that Jayson Blair took it upon himself to plant a tobacco field underneath Gregory Lynch's window.

Literary truth aims for something else, and the imaginary realms it provides access to do not require those describing them to literally go there. It requires less of a literal faithfulness to the real than a desire to produce a certain affective experience, to find the ways to bring it to life inside, and then, something that is difficult in another way, to share it with the reader.

~

This is the reason I feel that Jayson Blair should be absolved of many of the charges brought against him, even if the profession of journalist wasn't necessarily the one most suitable to exercising his talents.

Though shocking according to a certain logic, his attitude is also understandable if we translate it to a different value system, that of literature. His gradual decision to stop going to the places described in his reportages can also be defended, like that of other stay-at-home writers, by the care he took to maintain a proper distance between the places and the interviewees whose voices he wanted to be fully heard.

7

In Sporting Endeavors

(in which we wonder whether Philippides would
have used public transport after the Battle of
Marathon if given the opportunity)

LIKE ANTHROPOLOGY AND JOURNALISM, sport provides fertile
ground for those wishing to describe places they haven't been
to. If numerous sports take place in enclosed arenas and therefore aren't directly concerned, a substantial number of risky
practices like mountaineering, sailing or motor races, aeronau-
tical escapades or hunting in faraway countries[1] necessarily
lead their devotees to ask themselves whether it is worth throw-
ing themselves into a dangerous, exhausting venture if they can
instead limit their efforts to the essential and concentrate on
the story.

It is well within their interests to develop skills that will
allow them to speak with accuracy about a sporting
performance they have refrained from making and produce

---

1. See the example the eponymous Tartarin de Tarascon sets in Alphonse
Daudet's novel.

a convincing line about it that includes plenty of descriptions of the places they have been to, in order to remove all doubts from those suspecting that they may have taken a shortcut or stayed at home.

∼

In 1980, a woman by the name of Rosie Ruiz, a young American of Cuban origin, twenty-six years old, entered the annals of athletic history for two different reasons. The first one, purely sports related, was that she won the women's division in an important athletic challenge, the Boston Marathon, also setting the third-fastest time for a woman in any marathon.[2]

This event is one of the oldest distance races and one of the most famous in the world. It usually takes place on the third Monday in April. It has the characteristic of not being open to all candidates but only to preselected runners who have achieved a minimum qualifying time in another official marathon, ensuring an exceptional sporting standard.

It is still easy today to peruse the images that have survived of this historical course and the triumphant arrival of Rosie Ruiz. We discover a young woman in a yellow shirt, wearing the number W50, running the last few meters of the race with a stumbling stride before collapsing into the arms of spectators who help her, half-fainting, across the

---

2. VP+

line. After this, two policemen take over and support her under her arms to prevent her from collapsing entirely.

Next we see her answering a journalist's questions. Carrying the laurel wreath that right until 1986 was the only reward given to winners of this race and holding a silver cup, Rosie Ruiz, clearly in a state of euphoria, struggles to catch her breath and only briefly responds to the questions. Asked whether anyone helped her, she replied that she trained alone and was her own coach.

Rosie Ruiz's sporting performance was remarkable in any case because she ran the marathon in two hours, thirty-one minutes and fifty-six seconds, which was the best female time ever recorded at the Boston event and the third best time ever run by a woman in an official marathon. This fact alone made her an instant celebrity, something she was to remain.

∾

However, it wasn't Rosie Ruiz's exceptional time that brought her so much fame. She mainly went down in history for having lost her title again so quickly, after being accused of not actually having run the full course.

One of the things that attracted the organizers' attention was the exceptional time Rosie Ruiz made compared to her previous performance at the New York City Marathon. An even more revelatory indication in their eyes was the fact that the young woman recovered so rapidly after having crossed the finish line and could give no other explanation for her stunning physical condition than that she'd got up that morning brimming with energy.

Worse still, the officials sitting at various points around the race could not remember seeing the young woman pass by and wondered what mysterious, unknown path she had taken to be able to cover the distance between the start and the finish in record time.

The scandal reached greater proportions when the officials, looking into the New York Marathon—which had enabled Ruiz to qualify for the Boston event—became convinced, with witnesses to support it, that the young woman had covered part of the course by metro.

Accused of having cheated, Rosie Ruiz was disqualified from the Boston Marathon and the runner up, Jacqueline Gareau, was awarded the title. But Ruiz never admitted the fraud and continued to calmly affirm, despite all the evidence, that she had completed the legendary marathon in first place.

∽

I personally have difficulty understanding the reasons that lead the organizers to strip Rosie Ruiz of her title. As someone who is rather insensitive to sporting disciplines and remains perplexed by the idea of anyone spending part of their life trying to run a certain distance in a minimum amount of time, it isn't easy to understand the reproaches made to this young woman.

In terms of history, in any case, she doesn't seem to have lacked respect for the spirit of the marathon, which consisted of finding the best way of getting from one place to another in a limited amount of time. When Philippides ran from

Marathon to Athens to tell the Areopagus that the Persian army had been defeated, he chose the only method that was available to him, but it is obvious that he would have chosen a faster way if he'd had the opportunity.

In terms of sporting logic, aside from the fact that I doubt that using public transport is expressly forbidden in the marathon's rules, it would be naive to suppose that Rosie Ruiz was an isolated case. Other similar cases have been identified—suggesting that the number of frauds is actually quite high.[3] One only needs to leaf through the abundance of literature dedicated to exploits in inaccessible places with something of a critical mind to guess that some of these texts, like those of Marco Polo and Chateaubriand, were written at a fireside, and that the writers should be judged for their literary performance, not their sporting prowess.

The strangest thing about this story is that Rosie Ruiz was primarily reproached for her lack of imagination. The organizers considered it to her detriment that she was incapable of accurately describing certain parts of the route, in particular a girls' college that all the competitors should have passed—Wellesley College—whose students traditionally cheer with rapturous enthusiasm.

It is somewhat paradoxical that part of the charge against her was Rosie Ruiz's inability to describe the route, as if to criticize her refusal to resort to the particular kind of fiction—artistically fertile but unacceptable in sports—that is literary truth. The argument can easily be turned around

---

3. One celebrated case is that of the 1906 Tour de France, in which four cyclists were disqualified for taking the train from Nancy to Dijon.

because it would be just as easy to think that, if she'd really wanted to cheat, Rosie Ruiz would have gone to the trouble of gathering information on the route.

∽

As for myself, I would have no trouble, if asked, recounting the time I took part in the Boston Marathon some years ago.

For example, I have clear memories of the start of the race in the small town of Hopkinton, the gentle descent toward Ashland and going past the clock tower, then the train depot at Framingham, before skirting Lake Cochituate on our left and hearing, around the twenty-kilometer mark, the screams of the Wellesley students in the distance, carried by the wind.

How would it be possible to forget those groups of enthusiastic female students, frantically brandishing placards bearing inscriptions as encouraging as "I love you!" or "Marry me!" in front of the magnificent campus lost amid squirrel-filled trees. I can even give you a detailed description of the young blond woman wearing a blue suit and a red scarf who took it upon herself to run alongside me for several meters, spraying my face with a bottle of water.

And I can still remember, after we'd passed the park with the kangaroos, the hills before Newton, in particular the most difficult to climb, Heartbreak Hill, which precedes the prestigious Boston College, whose gothic tower spiked with four spires irresistibly reminds all Parisian competitors of the slender silhouette of the Saint-Jacques Tower.

Finally, I remember the route's gentle decline toward Boston after that last climb that heralds the Charles River, and how, although exhausted, my companions and I were transported by an increasing mass of spectators who were more and more enthusiastic the closer we got to the finish line, where we were taken into the care of an army of volunteers who carried us off to rest and regain our strength.

~

Despite appearances, Rosie Ruiz's fraud, if ever proven; the fantastical filter Marco Polo used to describe China to his beloved; and Margaret Mead reinventing the Samoan Islands with her playful young friends have more than one thing in common.

The first thing they have in common is the fact that we are talking about what I earlier called an imaginary realm, even if in one example a city is concerned. Undoubtedly we find ourselves faced with a different scenario than that of China or the Samoan Islands since a proliferation of concrete details is set against an abstract representation of loci here, reduced to a cord stretched across a finish line. But what the experiences do have in common is the rewriting of space, or, if one prefers, its *reconfiguration*, allowing the subjects to find themselves in a new place, more fulfilling in terms of fantasy.

The imaginary realm invented by Rosie Ruiz, where, like Peter Pan, she is capable of overcoming the laws of nature and achieving improbable sporting exploits, is modeled on that of childhood, whose privileges she redis-covers for a while. It is a realm where everything is possible: there are no barriers, no limits; dreams can rapidly become reality. It is a place where it is conceivable, for example, to transport oneself, without difficulty and seemingly without time, from one place to another in a city that has become a purely psychological space.

It is this experience of infantile omnipotence that Rosie Ruiz acts out in an imaginary place, completely constructed around the instant she triumphantly crosses the finish line to a cheering public, experiencing a jubilation that presum-ably resonates with the most distant of her experiences. There is neither distance nor time between desire and its realization in this fantasy space with its dreamlike construc-tion where the pleasure principle overrides the reality principle.

In both cases, this rewriting has an identical goal: to highlight the subject in a state of absolute pleasure. The amorous scenes with Chinese women dreamed up by Marco Polo and the multiple sexual encounters Margaret Mead imagines taking place over the entire Samoan Islands, trans-formed into a kind of primitive "general scene," are condensed in this moment of unique self-celebration, its intensity multiplied by the prism of the media, in absolute narcissistic happiness.

∿

So the example set by Rosie Ruiz shows how talk of imagi-nary realms cannot be understood without introducing a third notion corresponding to the unconscious life of the subject, that of the *inner landscape*.

Freud used this expression for a while to describe what was repressed in the mind, though finally it wasn't retained by psychoanalytic theory. "Repression," he wrote in his *Neue Folge der Vorlesungen zur Einführung in die Psychoanalyse* (1933), "is for me an inner foreign country (*inneres Ausland*), just as reality, if you will allow me to use an unusual expression, is an outer foreign country (*äusseres Ausland*)."[4]

Thus he evoked the image of an inner country or landscape and other related images like those of *regions and provinces*[5] in his search for tropes that would allow him to describe unconscious reality and the words best suited to showing it and thinking about it. It is an image that is a continuation of the propositions he often used to represent the interior of the psyche as a spatial form.

If the notion of an inner landscape is fitting, it is because it expresses how the interior of the psyche is certainly of a topological order, as Freud imagined and as Lacan further intuited with his idea of topology. It can also be thought of in geographical terms, with its landscapes, its elevations, its pits and even its inhabitants, which could include those

---

4. Sigmund Freud, *Neue Folge der Vorlesungen zur Einführung in die Psychoanalyse* [New Introductory Lectures on Psycho-Analysis] (Frankfurt am Main: Fischer Taschenburg Verlag, 1981), 50. Unfortunately, the recent Presses Universitaires de France translation has used the expressions "*territoire extérieur interne*" and "*territoire extérieur externe*."

5. "Superego, ego and id, these are the three empires, regions (*Gebiete*), provinces (*Provinzen*), between which we share the psychic apparatus of the individual, and now we are going to focus on their interrelationships." Ibid., 62.

parts of ourselves that seem to lead their own lives and, at times, be ready to seize autonomy at our expense.[6]

And it is to this fantasy image of an inner landscape that we refer to more or less consciously when we represent the insides of our minds like a region, a country or a city, open or fortified but separated from the others by frontiers that are more or less easy to cross and that assure our protection from the external world, even if we sometimes let down our barriers to certain privileged people.

The inner landscape, which might be another name for the unconscious, has both a collective and an unconscious dimension and is not isolated from the real world. On the contrary, it is behind the transformations to which we subject our representations of reality. And it is when the subject does not find peace there that he undertakes to substitute an imaginary world for the real one, whose geography is influenced by that of the inner landscape, becoming a place where he invents a realm that suits his needs.

If it isn't possible to know Rosie Ruiz's inner landscape with any accuracy—that is to say, her unconscious life with

---

6. Later in the text of *Neue Folge*, Freud constructs a complete allegory around the inner country and its different regions: "I imagine therefore a country whose terrain presents a varied configuration: there are hills, plains and lakes. The population is composed of Germans, Magyars and Slovaks performing various activities. Let us suppose the Germans, cattle-breeders, live on the hills, the Magyars, farmers and winegrowers, live on the plains, and the Slovaks, fishers and weavers, on the edge of the lakes. If this distribution was tidy and absolute, a Wilson would be delighted; geography would be easy to teach. But it is likely that when visiting the region, you would find less order and more confusion. Germans, Magyars and Slovaks sometimes live all mixed up, it is possible to have arable land on the hills and cattle on the plains." Ibid., 63.

its spaces and its inhabitants—we can still try to gain an idea from the traces left in her transformation of the real landscape of Boston into an imaginary realm, reduced in its totalitarian fiction to a space contracted around herself and her virtual exploit.

It is an inner realm that she would have complete mastery of and where she would also have control over space and time, as each of us secretly dreams. It is a place where she would rule without sharing, adored by subjects overwhelmed by admiration, retransmitting to her in a kind of infinite refraction that glorious image that certain self-obsessed rulers have others build for them in the form of statues in all the public spaces in their countries so as to have the pleasure, when walking, of being reflected back at themselves continually.

∼

As we can see, the reproach made to Rosie Ruiz of being incapable of accurately describing the route of the Boston Marathon can be understood in two different ways. First of all, it can be understood in the traditional way as a reproach for having tried to appropriate a title for herself that she had no right to.

But, according to a different kind of logic, it can also be understood as a reproach for not having been enough of a writer and not managing, by attaining that particular kind of truth that literature aims at, to reconfigure space in a sufficiently convincing manner for her readers and listeners to be able to accept it as their own and attempt to inhabit it in their minds.

8

In the Bosom of the Family

(in which we see how Emmanuel Carrère
manages to move a city to the edge of
a lake)

FAMILY LIFE, LIKE THE different professions we have just
examined, offers a number of notable situations in which the
ability to speak of places you haven't been to might be
required. At least two of these situations—in which it is
important to know how to make others believe that you were
elsewhere—are worth calling to mind.

The first is adultery. If led to describe his daily activities,
the person telling fibs to his official partner will necessarily
be obliged at some point to talk about places he hasn't been
to, since he is unable to talk about those he really went to at
that time.

The second, murder, is fortunately less common, but any
one of us might become confronted with the necessity of
having to take this route to ensure our peace and quiet one
day. The way of proving that you were somewhere other
than the place where the murder was committed has a

name, *an alibi*, and it is often crucial for the accused to be able to furnish one that seems valid.

The term *alibi* moreover could refer to the whole set of issues studied in this book if we think about it, since all armchair travelers go about things in the same way assassins do, situating themselves fictionally in a different place from wherever they were in reality.

∾

Many people know the terrible story of Jean-Claude Romand, the man who led his family and friends to believe for twenty years that he was a medical specialist, occupying an important position at the World Health Organization in Geneva, while in reality, he never made it through the second year of university.

Romand wasn't happy with just pretending to hold a prestigious medical position. He invented for himself—and without doubt ended up believing—a complete alternative existence in which he often traveled abroad, brushed shoulders with important figures in scientific research and politics and shone like a diamond in the salons and corridors of power.

To survive for such a long time without any income while living the kind of lifestyle befitting a medical specialist employed by an international organization, Romand was reduced to practicing scams—for example, divesting his family-in-law of all their savings by claiming to have invested them, and selling fake cancer medicines.

Curiously, during all those years, none of the people

close to Romand, nor anyone he came across or conversed with about his imaginary life, ever seemed to have noticed the improbability of his accounts, nor tried to verify what he said by inquiring at the WHO or consulting a medical directory, for example.

Yet sensing that the moment was approaching when he would be unmasked once and for all, and no longer able to handle his financial situation, Romand decided to bring his life to an end, as well as his wife's, his children's and his parents'. But, though he killed his relatives, he failed at his own suicide, was tried and given a nonreducible life sentence of a minimum of twenty-two years.

~

Just a few days after this multiple murder, the writer Emmanuel Carrère became interested in the Romand affair, which he had read about in the papers:

On the morning of Saturday, January 9, 1993, while Jean-Claude Romand was killing his wife and children, I was with mine in a parent-teacher meeting at the school attended by Gabriel, our oldest son. He was five years old, the same age as Antoine Romand. Then we went to have lunch with my parents, as Jean-Claude Romand did with his, whom he killed after their meal. I usually devote Saturday afternoons and Sunday to my family, but I spent the rest of that weekend alone in my studio because I was finishing a book I'd been working on for over a year, a biography of the science fiction writer

Philip K. Dick. The last chapter described the days he
spent in a coma before his death. I finished it on Tuesday
evening and on Wednesday morning opened my newspaper to the lead article on the Romand case.[1]

As the parallel between their two lives suggests, Emmanuel
Carrère soon felt moved to action by the Romand affair and
even came to experience a kind of fascination for the
murderer, expressed in the first letter he sent to him in prison,
six months later:

> I am a writer, the author to date of seven books; I
> enclose a copy of my latest work. Ever since reading
> about your case in the newspapers I have been haunted
> by the tragedy of which you were the agent and sole
> survivor.[2]

Although equally interested in setting up a meeting,
Romand, on his lawyer's advice, waited for the investigation
of his case to be closed before entering into correspondence
with Carrère and agreeing for the latter to write a book
about him.

Carrère then undertook to investigate the affair, reconstructed Romand's life and visited its primary locations,
followed the trial, met the murderer on several occasions

---

1. *L'Adversaire* (Paris: Les Éditions Gallimard, 2001), 9. Published in English as
The Adversary in a translation by Linda Coverdale (New York: Henry Holt,
2001).
2. Ibid., 36.

and, after many years of work which he almost abandoned due to the psychological stress of it all, managed to write and publish *The Adversary.*

~

In his book on the Romand affair, Emmanuel Carrère doesn't just reconstruct the murderer's life, he tries to get on the inside, taking advantage of his emotional closeness to the man to experience and have his reader experience what his protagonist felt. More than just an investigation, it becomes a simultaneous, double investigation Carrère makes not just into Romand, but also into himself.

During this quest, Emmanuel Carrère grows particularly interested in the periods that seemed to him to mark the essence of Romand's existence, namely the interminable days he was forced to spend away from home in complete indolence, due to the lack of a professional occupation:

In the beginning he went to WHO every day, later on less regularly. Instead of the road to Geneva, he'd take the one to Gex and Divonne or the one to Bellegarde, that leads to the motorway and Lyon. He'd stop at a news-stand to buy an armful of papers: dailies, magazines, scientific journals. Then he'd go and read them, either in a café—he was careful to change cafés often and to choose them far enough from home—or in his car. He would park in a carpark or at a service station and stay there for hours, reading, taking notes, dozing. He'd have a sandwich for lunch and continue reading throughout the afternoon in a different café, at a different service station.[3]

At other times, Romand prepared his virtual trips abroad and Carrère imagines scenes in which he researches places he hasn't been in order to be able to convincingly describe his travels to his family:

Lastly, there were the trips—conferences, seminars, symposiums, all over the world. He would buy a guide to the country; Florence would pack his suitcase. He'd drive off in his car, which he would supposedly leave in the long-term carpark at Geneva airport. In a modern hotel room, often near the airport, he would take off his shoes, stretch out on the bed, spend three or four days watching television and the planes taking off and landing outside his window.[4]

Romand didn't just buy travel guides for the countries he was supposed to be visiting. He put together the entire story of his trip in order to be believed by his loved ones when he returned:

He studied the guidebooks so he wouldn't make any mistakes in his stories when he got home. He tele-phoned his family every day to tell them what time it was and what the weather was like in São Paulo or

---

3. Ibid., 96.
4. Ibid., 97.

Tokyo. He'd ask how things were going in his absence. He'd tell his wife, his children, his parents that he missed them, was thinking of them, sent them a big kiss. He phoned no one else: whom would he have called? After a few days, he went home with presents bought in an airport gift shop. Everyone made a fuss over him. He was tired from jet lag.[5]

And so there are—aside from the interior place where he sought permanent exile—a multitude of imaginary realms that, during his alternative existence, Romand undertook to reinvent to maintain his wealthy identity and protect the bond he had with his loved ones from an unbearable reality.

≈

Even more than in the previous cases, we see how the opposition of real and imaginary places, and the partial or complete substitution of one for the other, only make sense when they are discussed in the context of that third space I suggested calling the "inner landscape," after Freud. Here in this case of absolute mythomania (compulsive lying), the inner landscape has become all pervasive.

Whereas in the previous examples, it only interfered with a limited part of the reality it played a part in distorting, here the inner landscape has become the subject's alternative reality and that of those close to them. Where Margaret Mead let herself go in a fantastical reverie about an imaginary

---

5. Ibid.

island, where Jayson Blair reconstructed places he might have been to, where Rosie Ruiz invented the ideal moment of bliss by erasing the surrounding space, Romand goes much further by forging all the parts of a second personality that allows him to survive. This second personality even becomes necessary, to the point of having to resort to murder when it risks being unmasked.

The same issue is at work in each of these different examples, whether the discourse on places these armchair travelers have not visited leads to success or to failure. For them it is a matter of finding, in greater or lesser denial of a disappointing reality, an ideal, fantasy place—that of the narcissistic pleasure an infant experiences in his mother's gaze and which is lost forever.   .

This unfindable ideal site of primitive pleasure, which we might call an *original place*, is something Romand won't stop trying to reinvent; he doesn't just limit himself to a single episode in his life but transforms the entire world in his mind to fit his purpose. We might suppose that he found shades of the lost bliss of the child in the dazzled eyes of his own children, filled with admiration like Wendy in *Peter Pan* as they listened to the tales of his heroic exploits on the other side of the world.

And it is no trivial matter that it was to his children—and to the child inside himself who hadn't wanted to grow up, we can surmise—that Romand recounted his travels to imaginary realms he'd never visited, as though he himself, like Peter Pan, hadn't managed to evolve, or feared that his children too would be confronted with the pain of becoming adults one day.

~

If I wholeheartedly support Margaret Mead's struggle to introduce libertinage to the Samoan Islands and Rosie Ruiz's attempt to legitimize the right to use public transport during sporting activities, if I can understand that Jayson Blair, under the influence of alcohol and drugs, described places in the United States he hadn't visited, there can obviously be no question of approving Jean-Claude Romand's behavior, especially once you know of its dramatic conclusion.

The fact remains that one can understand Carrère's fascination with Romand, a fascination that was so great he dedicated several years of his life to writing Romand's story and started to feel like he was losing his sanity. Interestingly enough, Romand has several things in common with writers, and in particular novelists. To start with, both handle *questions of identity* to a great degree. Just as novelists project themselves onto their imaginary characters, allowing themselves to limit denial to one area of their thoughts, Romand invented the entire persona of a great doctor, which he then acted out to perfection over many years. Similarly, the question of knowing who we are is something that has haunted Carrère for his entire literary career, starting with his early novel *The Mustache* (1987), and has since become its major theme.

Who are we, and more particularly, what is the nature of that dark side that threatens to engulf everything? Carrère recounts how Romand didn't really feel comfortable with him until he read his novel *La classe de neige*, a frightening story in which a child begins to realize, little by little, that his father is a murderer. But the question of knowing who we are is evidently not just about our internal dualities, it is also about the criminal potential that can arise in us in certain circumstances and whose uncontrollable power Romand experienced.

~

However, it is not just the question of identity that brings the two men together, it is also a form of *relationship to space*. Returning to his own passion for the Jean-Claude Romand case, Carrère suggests several times that there are commonalities between his life as a writer and the falsified existence of a killer, one of which is their relationship to place.

Evoking the endless days that Romand spent bored and alone—a duration of the kind that fascinates him, situated outside of any temporality—he proposes a significant parallel to the days spent by any writer:

I reread the letter he'd sent me with directions, I looked at the water, looked up at the grey sky to follow the flight of birds whose name I didn't know—I can't identify birds or trees and I find that sad. It was chilly. I started the engine to get some heat. The hot air made me sleepy. I thought about the studio where I go every morning after driving my children to school. This studio exists, people can visit me and phone me there. That's where I write and piece together screenplays that usually get filmed. But I know what it's like to spend all one's days unobserved: the hours passed staring at the ceiling, the fear of no longer existing. I wonder what he felt in his car? Pleasure? A mocking exultation at the idea of so masterfully fooling everyone around him? No, I was sure of that.[6]

In the passage that immediately follows this one, he evokes Romand's imaginary travels. Carrère explains that one of the places the fake doctor went to during his extratemporal peregrinations was the town of Divonne,[7] which is where one of his earlier novels, *Hors d'atteinte?*, is set, a novel that describes how a teacher slowly succumbs to a gambling obsession:

Divonne is a small spa near the Swiss border best known for its casino. I once used it as a setting for a few pages of a novel about a woman who lives a double life and tried to lose herself in the world of gambling. The novel was meant to be realistic and well-researched but, since I hadn't visited all the casinos I wrote about, I put Divonne on the shores of Lake Geneva when it's really about six miles away. There is actually something there referred to as a lake, but it's only a small sheet of water next to the place where Romand often parked. I parked there, too. It's the clearest memory I've kept of my first trip to the landscape of his life.[8]

---

6. Ibid., 99.
7. UP–
8. Ibid., 98.

In so doing, the writer rewrites the world and transforms it in the same way the mythomaniac killer does, albeit on a completely different scale. Both are confronted with the difficulty of inhabiting a space and neither of them succeeds in finding an adequate place—that is to say, a balance between the inner landscape and the real world—both of them finding themselves compelled to rewrite places in order to construct a makeshift identity.

Carrère's studio and Romand's car are *nonspaces* that they are forced to inhabit through professional necessity, but also because they respond to a profound psychological inability to invent an autonomous space that would allow them to establish their identity in a permanent manner.

Rewriting places, practiced to varying degrees by both of these men, has to do with the fact that they feel, probably more sorely than anyone else, that the space they inhabit deep down does not correspond to the real space that existence has led them to occupy, hence them finding themselves constantly driven to reshaping it in order to inhabit it.

The major difference between the two situations is that Carrère's empty studio, however anguishing it may be, is a place of research and self-exploration, while the car Romand uses to endlessly roam the roads for years is nothing but the burial chamber of an identity lost in the imaginary sparkle of his invented accounts.

≈

So we are dealing—writers undoubtedly more often than others—with complex spaces with indistinguishable boundaries that can only be imperfectly superimposed on the spaces of the real world, spaces we never stop transforming to suit our travels through our inner landscapes.

Based on the idea that writers, more than ourselves, live in aberrant spaces irreducible to real ones, I now propose in a final section to move on to some practical advice, taken from my long experience of armchair travel, for anyone finding themselves in a situation where they have to describe, for whatever professional or criminal reason, places they have never been to.

Procedures to Follow

9

Opening Up Frontiers

(in which we discover that the inhabitants of
Formosa get around on hippopotamuses and
rhinoceroses)

AFTER HAVING STUDIED THE different types of nonjour-
ney and some of the situations which might lead us to talk
about them, the time has come to put forward some sugges-
tions on how to acquit ourselves in such situations, which as
we've seen are more frequent than you might think, and
which each of us risks having to face at some moment or
other.

Seldom having traveled myself and already having found
myself having to talk about imaginary places on many an
occasion, I am not badly placed to offer some tips to those
who fear being confronted with the necessity of having to
reinvent space without being contradicted. And we can see
that far from falling victim to the situation, it is possible to
profit from it and gain a better knowledge of the places in
question and of oneself.

∼

At the beginning of the eighteenth century, an inhabitant of Formosa[1] called George Psalmanazar appeared in London and was an immediate sensation, rapidly gaining huge popularity.

He said he had been kidnapped from his island by Jesuits who had taken him to France and tried in vain to convert him to Catholicism. He spoke both Latin and English, and the religious persecution he'd suffered immediately won the hearts of the Anglican community in London, who took him under their wing.

Psalmanazar took it upon himself to promote his native island, largely ignored in Europe. He soon became very successful, partly because of his original style of dress—he wore exotic, baroque outfits—and his diet—he ate only raw meat—but above all for the novel information he was able to supply on his home country. His stories were mind-blowing.

His reputation grew even more after the 1704 publication of his work *An Historical and Geographical Description of Formosa, an Island Subject to the Emperor of Japan*. It had been preceded by an autobiography, which had swiftly been reprinted and was translated into several languages. The success of the book, which was due to the revelations it contained, led the author to give lectures to learned societies and increased his fame even more, not only in England but across Europe.

∽

It is true that Psalmanazar furnished a considerable amount of firsthand information on this country about which little

---

1. UP–

was known at the time. He made it known that Formosa, whose capital was Xternetsa, was a dependency of Japan and not of China, as had been incorrectly believed for a long time, and that the ruling regime was a monarchy.

Psalmanazar also provided some original insights into the country's customs. It was thanks to him that we learned that the inhabitants wore clothes that accurately reflected their social rank, that they were polygamous, that they ate their wives if they discovered them to be unfaithful and that human sacrifice was practiced regularly.[2]

We also discovered through Psalmanazar that the inhabitants of Formosa mainly ate snakes, that they lived underground in circular houses, and they didn't only use horses and camels to get around but also rode hippopotamuses and rhinoceroses.[3]

But Psalmanazar didn't content himself with providing precious information on life and customs on Formosa. He also allowed us to study its language.[4] Not only was he a fluent speaker, but he could also write it without difficulty. He explained that it used twenty characters, different from the characters used in China or Japan; it had six distinct

---

2. Psalmanazar's book, published in 1704, was reissued in 1705 in a new version that accentuated the cruelty of Formosa's morals. See the analysis of the two versions in Richard M. Swiderski's *The False Formosan: George Psalmanazar and the Eighteenth-Century Experiment of Identity* (San Francisco, CA: Mellen Research University Press, 1991), 66.

3. See Swiderski on Formosa's abundant fauna, which included lions, bears and wolves (ibid., 75).

4. For a detailed analysis of the language of Psalmanazar, see Michael Keevak, *The Pretended Asian: George Psalmanazar's Eighteenth-Century Formosan Hoax* (Detroit, MI: Wayne State University Press, 2004), 61.

tenses; and variations were made by using auxiliaries and tones.

In order to improve our knowledge, he was able to provide a translation of the Lord's Prayer which began with the words, "Amy Pornio dan chin Ornio vicy, Gnayjorhe sai Lory, Eyfodere sai Bagalin, jorhe sai domino apo chin Ornio." Formosa's language aroused keen interest among intellectuals, including Leibniz, and because of its rigor, continued to be studied by linguists decades after Psalmanazar's fraud had been brought to light.

∾

Of course Psalmanazar didn't come from Formosa. Born in France, he had adopted this ersatz identity after first having passed for an Irish pilgrim in order to travel around Europe more freely. He was happy to explain himself in his *Memoirs*, a book in which he recounted in detail the circumstances that led him to create this fiction.

Despite the success of his deception and the lack of criticism he received, it seems that Psalmanazar ended up feeling guilty about the way he had made fun of the English intelligentsia. While he didn't denounce himself during his lifetime, he dedicated himself to the study of theology and became a specialist in issues related to the Hebrew religion. It might be assumed that this was what led him to participate in a dictionary of religions for which he provided the entry on Formosa in which he criticized Psalmanazar's trickery, writing of himself in the third person.

When you think of the number of improbabilities with

which he embellished his stories, it is astonishing that Psalmanazar was able to construct this pretense and maintain it for several years. For example, there was the number of children he claimed were sacrificed each year on Formosa—twenty thousand—which led certain skeptical spirits to remark that at that rate, the population would rapidly become extinct.

Moreover, even if few people visited the island at that time, some Europeans did go there and their accounts were radically different from Psalmanazar's, who, with great composure, replied that they had only visited part of the island, never having ventured beyond the west coast.

The most surprising thing was that Psalmanazar, who had pale skin and blond hair, didn't correspond in the slightest to the picture one might have had of an inhabitant of Formosa. But the majority of his interlocutors didn't seem surprised by this—at that time, the concept of race wasn't decisive in the perception of otherness. And Psalmanazar explained eruditely that members of the intellectual class on the island were pale skinned because they lived underground.

≈

How did Psalmanazar go about fooling so many people? The first reason he managed to convince so many intellectuals and for such a long period of time was the verisimilitude of his description of Formosa and his own personal investment in the simulation.

With Psalmanazar, we rediscover the play of intertwined

places that I noted earlier. For the real country of Formosa, which was difficult to visit at the time, Psalmanazar substituted an imaginary country that he knew how to reinvent in every aspect without ever having been there. But this substitution doesn't become intelligible until we take into account what I proposed calling the "inner landscape" of the author and the eternally lost "original place" that he never stops searching for in vain through all of his confabulations, just like every one of us.

It is notable in fact that Psalmanazar, by engaging in this deception, isn't only looking for the tangible social benefits he might gain from describing a virtually unknown land; he also attempts to construct a true romance of his origins by inventing for himself a new identity and a new history, going so far as to develop a new language whose rules he had better know, given that he is the only person in the world who can speak it.

To this end, Psalmanazar's Formosa is a compromise formation in the Freudian sense, like a dream or a delirium. Psalmanazar recreates himself through an imaginary Formosa that allows him to deploy an infantile fantasy of omnipotence—just as Rosie Ruiz and Jean-Claude Romand did in their own ways. He invents his own origins and those of everyone close to him and creates a comprehensive family saga of which he is the hero.

∼

Psalmanazar's second quality is the possession of a fertile imagination. In this, he fits into the tradition of authors like

Marco Polo and Margaret Mead's female informants—like them he is capable of inventing a plethora of picturesque elements that capture and retain the public's attention.

It is impossible to hope to speak with any conviction of places you haven't been to without a vivid imagination. The capacity to dream and to make others dream is essential to anyone wanting to describe an unknown place and hoping to capture the imagination of their readers and listeners.[5]

This imagination is deployed in several ways that appear contradictory. First of all, Psalmanazar invents a country to suit his taste, gives it a political system, an economy, a language, customs, and even endows it with a unique animal husbandry. What he constructs is a complete world, capable of functioning, like the imaginary realms that populate travelogues and children's games.

This imagination relies upon a strong sense of faux realism, or what one might call *true detail*. Like Chateaubriand, with his detailed descriptions of the flowers and insects of parts of America that he took good care not to explore, Psalmanazar nurtures the tiniest elements of his stories to create a credible illusion of an alternative reality.

But, as specific as it is, the place invented by Psalmanazar cannot clearly be situated in any particular locality. Although

---

5. And Psalmanazar does it with enough conviction to win the support of his interlocutors. In his *Memoirs*, he tells how he had resolved that, once having made an assertion, he would never to go back on it, whatever unlikelihood might be revealed or contradiction made by witnesses (George Psalmanazar, *Memoirs of* ★★★★. *Commonly Known by the Name of George Psalmanazar; a Reputed Native of Formosa. Written by Himself in Order to Be Published after His Death* (Farmington Hills, MI: Gale Ecco Print Editions, Dublin, 2011), 141.

it has a determined geographical location, it could just as easily be found *anywhere at all*. The truth is that Psalmanazar combined several travelogues from different continents, and his montage contains elements from the Aztec and Inca civilizations—starting with human sacrifices—as well as from the Japanese and Chinese.[6]

It is no trivial matter that Psalmanazar transports hippopotamuses and rhinoceroses to Formosa, anticipating Henri Michaux's gesture when he added camels to his description of Honfleur.[7] Transporting animals or objects from one country to another, prevalent in the accounts of armchair travelers, shows that there is a different kind of space here than the one that prevails in the real world, *a place that is much more flexible and mobile than the one in which we operate on a daily basis*.

This apparently contradictory mixture of precision and ambiguity is essential to the invention of a haven of refuge conducive to the imagination. The details guarantee the existence of the imaginary place and the veracity of the account; the ambiguity allows the reader or listener to project themselves individually according to a particular hook offered by

---

6. Formosa's language is a montage, too. Its articles (*oi hic, ey haec, ai hoc*) are inspired by Latin (see Swiderski, 75).

7. "In the past I had too much respect for nature. I placed myself in front of things and landscapes and I let them be.

That's over, from now on I'm going to *intervene*.

I was at Honfleur and I was bored. So I resolutely added some camels. It wasn't really called for. Never mind, it was my idea. Besides, I went about this with the greatest prudence. I introduced them first of all on very busy days, on Saturdays in the marketplace." Henri Michaux, *La nuit remue* (Paris: Les Éditions Gallimard, 1967). English translation by Michele Hutchison.

the account and to find a singular space that chimes with their own inner landscape.

∽

But personal investment and imagination would not have been sufficient to explain—any more than in Margaret Mead's case—that such an absurd fiction could be sustained for so long and accepted by the scientific community like a realist document. A model of individual compromise, Psalmanazar's Formosa is also, when you take a closer look, a model of collective compromise.

If you think about it, the description of Formosa is just as much a plural work as a singular fiction. As we have already seen, the conversations we can have about places we don't know do not only concern the places and ourselves, but also involve the people we are addressing ourselves to, often benevolent accomplices.

Michael Keevak showed in the book he wrote on Psalmanazar that the latter's success can be explained by the fact that Psalmanazar addressed a disquisition to the English that they wanted to hear, particularly in terms of religion, and offered them an image of themselves that they found recognizable:

Psalmanazar, in short, wasn't just the perfect response to the start of a period of fascination for exotic chinoiseries, but also the solution to a growing desire amongst Europeans to meet exotic specimens who weren't overly exotic: as Linda Lomeris wrote, foreigners should function as a kind of mirror of the subjective preoccupations of

Europeans. Psalmanazar might have been a stranger who ate raw meat and spoke a completely foreign language, but he didn't present the slightest menace. After all, he was a noble savage, he was Anglican, and (in particular?) he was white.[8]

Psalmanazar's Formosa functioned as a collective compromise in the sense that it allowed an entire community—who weren't necessarily, on the unconscious plane, as fooled as they led us to believe—to think about their relationship to a remote foreign country. As such, this fiction allowed real psychological work to be done, in the same way that Margaret Mead's imaginary Samoans offered Americans a transitional place onto which they could project their unconscious desires and be a step ahead in thinking about sexual liberation.

Hence the importance of the *spatial jamming* that Psalmanazar engages in by presenting a place that is just as specific as it is unsuitable. His rewriting of Formosa is all the more liable to please a vast audience because it isn't too limited geographically, nor too personal in terms of fantasy, but caters to all. In doing this, he places Formosa in the universalized space of a collective mythology in which numerous readers can find themselves.

∼

The bric-a-brac country that Psalmanazar constructs with the support of his benevolent audience shows that, like

---

8. Michael Keevak, *The Pretended Asian*, 53.

numerous armchair travelers, he doesn't play with the real geographical place addressed by science, but with an aberrant space that is the same as the one literature invents to describe the world.

This aberrant space is resolutely *atopic*—that is to say, it doesn't experience the limitations that organize the geography of the real world. It possesses great mobility, like dreams do, dominated as it is in the same way by the primary processes of the unconscious. It is possible to move at full speed from one location to another as Rosie Ruiz did, as though no distance was insurmountable.

It establishes communication between geographical places that are not adjacent to each other in the real world but separated by large distances by renewing the frontiers. It is therefore not surprising that in this space, animals are able to move without difficulty from one continent to another and settle in new territories where one would never come across them normally.

And it is equally likely that, profiting from the mobility of the literary space and this opening of frontiers that disrupts circulation in the real world, the characters of certain works of fiction profit from this by passing from one text to another and settling in a world that seems more hospitable to them.

If we don't take into account the atopic character of literary space, we cannot hope to understand the extent to which it involves a different space from that of the real world, nor grasp the multitude of discrete events that occur, sometimes without even the writer's knowledge, and which merit our attention.

～

Paying attention to the atopic character of literary space is essential when describing places you haven't been to, since this atopia and the new traffic rules it establishes between worlds encourage a generous opening up of the field of descriptions by no longer limiting them to a single evoked area.

In fact, it encourages supplementing described areas with elements borrowed from other real or imaginary worlds as Psalmanazar does, elements that it might be desirable to have in the story in order to make the descriptions of the place one hopes to have others experience more sensitive and relevant.

Time Travel

(in which one sees, through Karl May, that a good
way of talking about the American West is by
moving it in time)

THE NECESSARY CONDITIONS FOR being able to talk perti-
nently about places you haven't been to are knowing how to
reinvent space in an imaginative way, and not hesitating to
blur the usual boundaries in order to remodel it and make it
more open.

But this reinvention of space isn't necessarily all it takes
to produce a discourse that can host the fantasies and reveries of the majority. Fully developing its dynamism also
involves being able to extract from the traditional categories
of temporality those that constitute an obstacle to creativity
and to understanding the world through the limits they
impose on perception.

∽

European literary history has not given as much credit as

was deserved to the German writer Karl May, who was born in 1842 and died in 1912. He was one of his country's most widely read writers and remains the subject of a real cult there. A symbol of German culture as much as Goethe and Schiller, he is revered by intellectuals from opposing political poles who nevertheless manage to find themselves in his vision of the world.

Karl May's life actually resembled a Karl May popular novel.[1] He was born into a very poor family—four of the fourteen children would die in infancy—and suffered from blindness caused by malnutrition shortly after his birth. He regained his sight at the age of six, but suffered a severe upbringing from a violent father who abused him. Highly intelligent, he managed to break free from his background and successfully complete his schooling.

In 1861, when he was studying to become a teacher, he was accused of stealing a watch from his roommate and sent to prison, thereby losing any chance he had of a career in public service. Next he committed a number of petty thefts and was sentenced to four years of prison in 1865, to be released in 1868 for good conduct. Imprisoned again in 1869, he managed to escape. He was recaptured in 1870 and sentenced to four more years of prison. He was released in 1874 but remained under police observation and was not able to travel freely around Germany.

In November 1874, he published his debut novel, *The Rose*

---

1. This biographical section was inspired by a now-defunct website dedicated to Karl May: http://www.karl-may-stiftug.de/.

of Ernstthal, followed in 1875 by several works that included the first adventures of the hero who would ensure his celebrity, the Indian Winnetou, launching himself into an abundant and regular production of novels. In 1876, he met the woman who would become his wife in 1880, Emma Pollmer. In 1879, he went to prison again for three weeks for having posed as an investigator.

His success grew from the 1880s onward, in particular with the Asian adventures of Kara Ben Nemsi, and most of all, the American adventures of Winnetou and his friend Old Shatterhand, a trilogy dedicated to the duo that appeared in 1893. In 1896, he acquired two guns, the "silver shotgun" and the "bear killer" that would figure in his books and had himself photographed as Old Shatterhand and Kara Ben Nemsi. The legend of Old Shatterhand began to grow, and numerous Karl May clubs were created.

In 1899, he traveled through the Orient for several months with his wife, venturing as far as Sumatra and passing through Beirut and Jerusalem. He got divorced in 1903, having fallen in love with the widow of a friend, Klara Plöhn, who he took to visit the United States in 1908. As his success grew, both in Germany and internationally, he became the subject of fierce attacks and was accused of corrupting morals.

≈

A large number of Karl May's books, presented as autobiographies, were written in the first person, and May always claimed to have personally experienced the adventures he wrote about. He made no bones about the fact that he was the narrator in the adventures of Winnetou and that Old Shatterhand was the nickname people had given him in the West. In order to increase the verisimilitude of his account, he decorated his sumptuous villa with souvenirs brought back from his numerous travels.

In reality, Karl May set foot in North America for the first time in 1908, four years before his death. Accompanied by his second wife, he visited New York, Albany, Buffalo and Niagara Falls. But he prudently avoided traveling to the American West,[2] which he had introduced to the German public and which they had grown fond of, limiting his itinerary to the large American cities of the north and east.

His lack of direct experience with the American West was compensated by his use of many documentary sources, including the novels of James Fenimore Cooper—starting with *The Last of the Mohicans*, whose influence on European adventure novels was considerable—which he had read in prison and which had inspired him to write.

But he was particularly assisted in his work by an abundant imagination that rendered traveling to the place unnecessary and allowed him to invent, as Psalmanazar did, an imaginary realm all the more plausible because it was based on the testimonies of numerous reliable informants who had taken the risk of venturing out into the field.

---

2. VP++

～

However, Karl May didn't content himself with propounding a substitute universe for our world; he took it upon himself to improve it. The tableau he offers of the conquest of the West actually goes further than the usual representations, in the first instance in the way he inverts the stereotypes attached to the whites and the Indians.

The hero of the Winnetou adventure series, who is also the narrator, is a white man of colossal strength nicknamed Old Shatterhand. The first volume of the series tells how he decided, when living on the East Coast and driven by curiosity and a taste for adventure, to head out west and was hired as a railway engineer whose job it was to get things ready for the construction of the new route. His physical strength, which allowed him, for example, to effortlessly slay a grizzly bear or capture a mustang, was admired by all. Within the railway team, however, tensions were rife, and the narrator, who had one faithful friend, Sam Hawkens, attracted the animosity of one of the men of the group, Rattler.

An encounter with the Apache tribe, who are protesting against the construction of the railway on their land, raises tensions even more. During a discussion with them, the drunken Rattler kills the tribe's wise man, Kleki-Petrah, without any apparent reason. The Indians, led by their chief, Intschu-Tschuna, and his son, Winnetou, leave without fighting but are followed by the whites who fear retaliation and who, assisted by the Kiowas, a rival tribe to the Apaches, draw them into a trap and capture the chief and his son.

Hearing that the Indian chiefs are about to be killed, which goes against the agreement they have with the Kiowas, Old Shatterhand frees them under cover of darkness, without their being able to see their rescuer's face. He is captured by the Apaches a short time later, in the company of Sam Hawkens and Rattler. After having sentenced him to death, the Indians recognize his good faith and execute only Rattler. They then propose that Old Shatterhand joins them, and Winnetou and the narrator drink each other's blood to seal their union.

∾

The seemingly stereotypical plot of the novel should not obscure the inversion of its representation of the races. Old Shatterhand, impregnated with Christian morality and a sense of honor, is certainly a positive hero, but a large number of the whites around him and with whom he works, starting with the assassin Rattler, are presented in a very negative manner.

The representation of the Indians is not at all uniform since the Kiowas are depicted as thieves who break their word. But the Indians in the foreground, the Apaches, appear as honorable men, courageous[3] and trustworthy, and desirous

---

3. To punish Rattler for having killed Kleki-Petrah, the Indians decide to torture him. But, once they begin, Rattler emits such terrible cries that the Indians unfasten him. They feel a coward doesn't deserve to be tortured and condemn him instead to swim across a dangerous river in which he drowns.

of peace. And the hero who gave his name to the series, Winnetou, is a sympathetic figure.

The character who best embodies the inversion of traditional representations is Kleki-Petrah, a kind of guru to the Indians, infinitely respected by them and whose assassination by Rattler is at the heart of the plot. He presents himself to the whites as an Apache before telling them that he's actually a German who settled in the United States, but, disgusted by the whites, decided to switch sides:

> I fled the world and men to do penance and turned towards the wilderness. I saw the wrongs done to the Indians, and my heart overflowed with wrath and compassion. I resolved to atone for my wrongdoings and those of the White man by devoting myself to the Indians.[4]

In general, and even if neither of the two groups here are monolithic, the Indians are presented in a much more favorable light than the whites. In Karl May's books they aren't murderous savages as literary tradition maintained for a long period of time, but beings close to nature who feel condemned to extinction and who merit respect and consideration.

But the inversion of stereotypes doesn't only involve the point of view of the characters and the peoples; its primary concern is the overall policy of the whites in North America. The book is actually very critical of the way the Europeans seized Indian land, disregarding their rights. As early as the

---

4. Karl May, *Winnetou: The Apache Knight*, trans. Marion Ames Taggart (General eBooks, 2012), 14. Revised English translation by Michele Hutchison.

first encounter between the railway engineers and the
Apaches, the latter become the spokespersons for a people
robbed of their property without the slightest consultation:

"I'd like my white brother to answer one question
truthfully. Do you have a house?"

"Yes."

"With a garden?"

"Yes."

"If a neighbor cut a path through that garden would
my brother allow it?"

"No."

"The lands beyond the Rocky Mountains and to the
east of the Mississippi belong to the pale faces. What
would they say if the Indians built a railroad there?"

"They would drive them away."

"My white brother has answered truthfully. But the
pale faces turn up on these lands of ours and drive away
our mustangs and kill our buffalo; they look for gold and
precious stones, and now they are going to build a long,
long road on which their fire-horses can run. More pale
faces will follow this road, and settle among us, and take
the little we have left. What must we to say to this?"[5]

The Indian chief, Intschu-Tschuna, continues along these
lines, making reference to the religion the whites lay claim to
without respecting its teachings:

---

5. Ibid., 13.

"Do we have fewer rights than they do? You call yourselves Christians and speak of love, yet you say: 'We can rob and cheat you, but you must be honest with us.' Is that love? You say that your God is the Father of all men, whether their skins are red or white. Is he only our stepfather? Are we nothing but adoptive sons? Didn't all the land belong to the Indians? It has been taken from us and what have we been given instead? Misery, misery, misery. You drive us farther and farther back and force us closer and closer together and soon we shall be suffocated."[6]

Not only does the text give the Indians a voice, the narrator does not hide the fact that they are well within their rights when they oppose European colonization:

He cast me a scornful glance and said to Kleki-Petrah in a contemptuous tone: "Your teachings sound good, but they do not often tally with what I see. Christians deceive and rob the Indians. Here is a young pale face with a brave heart, an open face, honorable eyes, and when I ask what he is doing here he tells me he has come to steal our land. The faces of the white men are good and bad, but inside they are all the same."

To be honest, his words filled me with shame. Could I be proud of my participation in this matter—I, a Catholic, who had been taught at a young age: "Thou

---

6. Ibid., 13.

shalt not covet thy neighbor's goods?" I blushed for my race and for myself, faced with this fine savage . . .[7]

Kleki-Petrah is so ashamed of himself and his people that he decides to break from them for good—it is hard to imagine a more violent condemnation of the contradiction between the precepts of Christianity and the reality of the white man's customary practices.

∾

If we summarize the vision of the American West in the Winnetou series, we might say that the Indians are not inferior to the whites; they are more respectful of the codes of honor and less corrupt; and the whites dispossessed them of their land by illegal expropriation with a determination akin to genocide. It can't be said that this representation of the creation of modern North America was dominant in Europe at the end of the nineteenth century, and especially not during the first half of the twentieth century.[8]

So the idea that the Indians fought for the land that had been stolen from them was popularized in the nineteenth century by a German writer who had never set foot in America, in the same way that Phileas Fogg protected a

---

7. Ibid., 12.

8. In terms of art, if one takes into account the privileged vehicle of the Western representation of Indians, we have to wait until 1950 and Delmer Daves's film *Broken Arrow* to see an inversion of the dominant representation of Indians as popularized in John Ford's *Stagecoach*.

woman threatened with murder without knowing anything about India. In the absence of travel, May must have been able to seek inspiration in the novels of James Fenimore Cooper, starting with *The Last of the Mohicans*, which humanely presented the Indians in a favorable light. But Cooper didn't at all support the idea that the Indians were victims of colonialism and that their combat was legitimate.

May's vision is all the more original because he isn't satisfied with just describing a reality he condemns. He also suggests the path to a possible transformation. Old Shatterhand, the author's official representative, is not only critical of the attitudes of the whites toward the Indians, he also tries to change the balance of power in favor of the victims of dispossession.

Of course it isn't a good idea to idealize May's vision of the conflict between the Europeans and the Indians. In spite of the respect he shows for the latter and his denunciation of the injustices they suffered, the reader still gets the feeling that European civilization is superior in his eyes. It is no trivial matter that in the final volume in the Winnetou trilogy, the Indian dies after having converted to Christianity. But the fact remains that the imaginary realm May invents functions as a personal and collective laboratory, allowing the relationships between the different factions fighting for land in North America to be rethought.

～

Unlike the participatory observation that Karl May was so fiercely opposed to, observation from a distance not only permits the invention or reinvention of the world but allows it to be transformed through writing, rendering it more just.

Making the world fairer doesn't just imply modifying it in a Christian or Marxist way and fighting against economic and social inequalities or ensuring that criminals are punished. The writer can hope to situate her world-transforming intervention on an entirely different plane—even if the two meanings of the word "transforms" are not incompatible.

The writer shouldn't be concerned with justice in its own right but with doing justice to the facts. This doesn't come down to simplifying the real, as is often the case with radical transformative ideologies, but on the contrary, to lending it a superior form of complexity while still making it readable.

It is also noteworthy that Winnetou refrains from offering solutions to a problem that does not have any. There can be no real compromise between the Apaches' legitimate claim to the land that belongs to them and the obligation Old Shatterhand has to the railway company that has employed him. The compromise suggested by the Apache chief, which aims at a friendly gesture to pacify the relationship between Old Shatterhand and his new friends, is not a solution:

"I can finish my work then?" I asked, touched by such generosity.

"Yes."

"It means that you consent to the theft."

"Not to the theft, only to the survey. The lines you

make on paper do us no harm; the theft only begins when the pale faces' workers come to build the road for their fire-horse."[9]

The sophisticated solution proposed by the Apache chief—which acknowledges that the surveying of their lands and the mapping out of the railway are not yet a dispossession and that this will only really begin with the arrival of the workers—doesn't seem to resolve anything and does not stop the war. But it clashes with the discourse of hatred by substituting it with a complex discourse characterized by listening to the Other.

≈

Not having his gaze fixed on the Wild West—and there was no risk of that happening, since he'd taken care never to go there—allowed Karl May to see *beyond* the real place, and this beyond means not only beyond space, but also beyond time. The tolerant country he describes where Old Shatterhand and Winnetou exchange blood and seek an impossible conciliation does not correspond to the real country he would have encountered had he traveled there in person. It corresponds to what this country potentially could be and effectively became, at least in part, a century later when the crimes the Indians were subjected to were recognized.

---

9. Ibid., 49.

Similarly, when he visited the ancient ruins, Chateaubriand didn't stop at the contingent appearance of the places his guide was so keen to have him visit but tried to grasp them in a chronological movement opposite to that of Karl May, projecting himself centuries back[10] and seeing with his own eyes, beyond the deceptive illusion of the anecdote, the ancient town that had once stood at this place and which in a certain sense had never stopped existing for the writer.

Just as it is a different place, the imaginary realm also falls under a different time, since it is based both on the writer's unconscious and on that of the place described. Its mobility derives not only from the fact that it is made up of disconnected fragments of places, linked as they would be in a dream, but also because it belongs to different periods of time that a real writer is capable of synthesizing in an enlightening manner, in defiance of chronology.

In describing the awareness of the collective crime Europeans of good faith are in the process of committing, Karl May plagiarizes in advance the artists and historians of a century later who will undertake, after a dark period of caricature of the Indian claims, to expose the despoilment and mass murders upon which the edifice of the United States was based.[11]

---

10. Or forward, like when Chateaubriand, unable to see the archaeological site at Corinth since he didn't go there, described the town as it would be in several centuries, extracting it from any temporality.

11. See Pierre Bagard, *Le Plagiat par anticipation* (Paris: Les Éditions de Minuit, 2009).

Thus, speaking of places you haven't been to doesn't only require imagination but also supposes a perception of space in its temporal dimension, that is to say, in its essential chronological mobility, a mobility that allows it to belong simultaneously to several periods, and whose transitory reunion writing illuminates and deepens.

∼

The improvement Karl May subjected America's Wild West to does not occur exclusively in literature. The new stereotypes he helped create through the considerable success of his works imposed themselves little by little on the collective unconscious, notably through that extraordinary vehicle for transforming stereotypes, the western.

And if we admit that routes of transmission are sometimes strange and nonlinear,[12] we can also ask ourselves whether this writer, who had never set foot in the American West, didn't manage in the end, through the work he effected on the imagination, to change the image the Europeans and the North Americans had of the Indians, thereby transforming the relationship between these peoples on a long-term basis.

---

12. See the works of Georges Didi-Huberman, in particular "The Surviving Image: Aby Warburg and Tylorian Anthropology," *Oxford Art Journal* 25, no. 1 (2002): 59–69.

Through the Mirror

(in which Blaise Cendrars shows us how to take
the most famous train in the world by staying at
the station)

REMOVING THE PLACE YOU want to describe from the double constraints of space and time renders it unsuitable, thereby increasing the chances of you being able to share it with your readers and open it up to the pluralistic play of collective fantasy.

But the function of the writer who expresses himself by spoken word or writing cannot be limited to the creation of this imaginary realm. It also involves him being capable, as with a real journey, of transporting his readers by giving them the feeling that they have left their usual domicile and have been transported to the other side of the mirror where they can reside in that domain, having broken free of their moorings to actual geography.

≈

If there is one prime example of a traveling writer in French twentieth-century literature, it has to be Blaise Cendrars, who titled one of his books *Bourlinguer*—roaming—for a reason.

An indefatigable traveler in his youth, the French writer of Swiss origin always mixed traveling with writing, a fact that allows us to discover through his fiery poetic prose many far-off lands rendered familiar by his enterprise— both in his fictional biographies like *Rhum* and *Gold* and in his autobiographical works.

Cendrars left Switzerland at a very young age, possessed by an irrepressible desire for adventure. After receiving a devastating school report, the future writer decided in 1904 to run away from home and headed toward Germany and then Russia.[1] He got to know a businessman who took him with him on the Trans-Siberian Express,[2] the famous train linking Moscow to Vladivostok over more than nine thousand kilometers, whose construction was almost complete.

In the opinion of Cendrars's biographers, who include his daughter, Miriam, this journey was an extraordinary experience from which he returned transformed. He reviewed the journey several years later, in 1913, in the poem "The Prose of the Trans-Siberian," which marked just as much a crucial step forward for twentieth-century poetry as his friend Apollinaire's "Zone" did.

Despite its relatively elliptical character, this long prose text doesn't only pay testament to the force of this foundational

---

1. See Miriam Cendrars, *Blaise Cendrars: L'or d'un poète* (Paris: Les Éditions Gallimard, 1996), 24.
2. DP+-

experience, it also offers us a series of valuable snippets of information: on the Russia of 1914, which was at boiling point, and on the material conditions experienced by those who had decided to take this legendary train, sometimes at their peril.

∽

Cendrars's poem, whose full title is "The Prose of the Trans-Siberian and of Little Jeanne of France," begins in Moscow, where the poet arrived at the age of sixteen. Nine years later, he recalls it thus:

> Back then I was still young
> I was barely sixteen but my childhood memories were
>   gone
> I was 48,000 miles away from where I was born
> I was in Moscow, city of a thousand and three bell
>   towers and seven train stations
> And the thousand and three towers and seven stations
>   weren't enough[3]

Taking this as his point of departure, the poet interweaves several strands. First of all, he undertakes to describe, as expected, some of the traditional sights of the Russian plains as seen through the window of the moving train:

---

3. Translation by Ron Padgett, *Nowhere Magazine* (April 2011), http://nowheremag.com/2011/04/the-prose-of-the-trans-siberian-and-of-little-jeanne-of-france-blaise-cendrar/.

The rain falling
The peat bogs swelling
Siberia turning
Heavy sheets of snow piling up
And the bell of madness that jingles like a final desire
   in the bluish air
The train throbs at the heart of the leaden horizon
And your desolation snickers . . .[4]

These descriptions of the countryside are accompanied by sentimental evocations—Cendrars recounts his encounter with a young woman who becomes his occasional interlocutor and to whom he regularly addresses himself for the length of the poem:

Tears rise from the bottom of my heart
If I think, O Love, of my mistress;
She is but a child, whom I found, so pale
And pure, in the back of a bordel.

She is but a fair child who laughs,
Is sad, doesn't smile, and never cries;
But the poet's flower, the silver lily, trembles
When she lets you see it in the depths of her eyes.[5]

A large part of the poem is thus organized around an address to a mysterious, unidentifiable young woman, who

---

4. Ibid.
5. Ibid.

does not remain mute and asks the same insistent question several times:

"Blaise, say, are we really a long way from Montmartre?"[6]

To these first two descriptive and sentimental strands, a historical strand is added in the form of scattered notes on the Russo-Japanese War, which was happening at the time in Siberia and whose images of desolation—which obviously marked the writer—multiply toward the end of the poem, giving it a significantly more serious tone:

> I saw
> I saw the silent trains the black trains returning from
>   the Far East and going by like phantoms
> And my eyes, like taillights, are still trailing along
>   behind those trains
> At Talga 100,000 wounded were dying with no help
>   coming
> I went to the hospitals in Krasnoyarsk
> And at Khilok we met a long convoy of soldiers gone
>   insane
> I saw in quarantine gaping sores and wounds with
>   blood gushing out
> And the amputated limbs danced around or flew up in
>   the raw air
> Fire was in their faces and in their hearts[7]

---

6. Ibid.
7. Ibid.

Note finally—something that makes reading the text even more complicated—that the journey is not recounted in a linear fashion and that other countries traversed by the poet, like Belgium, Italy or America, and other time periods, like his childhood, interfere with the account, which features both atopism and anachronism, and therefore distances itself from any real geographical reference:

All those faces glimpsed in the stations
All the clocks
Paris time Berlin time Saint Petersburg time all those
    stations' times
And at Ufa the bloody face of the cannoneer
And the absurdly luminous dial at Grodno
And the train moving forward endlessly
Every morning you set your watch ahead
The train moves forward and the sun loses time
It's no use! I hear the bells
The big bell at Notre-Dame
The sharp bell at the Louvre that rang on Saint
    Bartholomew's Day
The rusty carillons of Bruges-the-Dead
The electric bells of the New York Public Library
The campaniles of Venice[8]

∽

8. Ibid.

The intersection of these different themes and the confusions of places and times tends to disorientate the reader and give him the feeling that the poem is based upon a series of random associations, like the practice of the surrealists a few years later, who were actually inspired by Cendrars's free verse.

But the poem's originality doesn't stop here. More than a text, it should really be spoken of as a text-object, since when the artist Sonia Delaunay met Cendrars at their mutual friend Apollinaire's house, she proposed creating a work of her own that would enter into dialogue with the poem. She then undertook to depict a two-meter "accordion," whose color representations would run alongside and comment on Cendrars's text.

As such, the real work, difficult to reproduce and which only exists in a few copies, is in reality composed of these two associated works—arising from two different art forms, called into play as complementary objects. Ideally one should follow their progress together to perceive the deep logic and the exchanges of resonances.[9]

The essential thing that the painting contributes to the text is a kind of scansion, already active in the poem thanks to the versification, but which is accented by the presence and the dynamic play of the colors, lending a rhythm to the reading process like the jolting of a train along a track would do for a writer.

Having a different rhythm from that of the text since

---

9. A complete reproduction can be found at the beginning of Miriam Cendrars's *Blaise Cendrars: L'or d'un poète*, op. cit.

there is no direct correspondence between the words and the images, Sonia Delaunay's abstract designs—which on occasion reveal identifiable forms like the red Eiffel Tower that accompanies the final lines—devise a different rhythm and even manage to mix with the text at times, in large splotches of color that cross the boundary between the two creations.

~

Having taken the Trans-Siberian Express myself, I can in any case testify to the accuracy of Cendrars's vision of Russia, as one can see it go past today, more than a century after his maiden voyage, from the luxury compartments of the most famous train in the world.

How could one not recognize Moscow, even more than a century later, in the evocative representation that the poet provides through his network of metaphors, his depiction of forests of bell towers and his description of the Kremlin, which he compares to an immense Tartar cake whose surrounding churches suggest almonds?[10]

And similarly, how can we not believe in the descriptions that he gives us of his long journey through Siberia and how can we not share his feeling—when faced with these plains lost in the rain, snow and peat, populated by herds of antelopes and interspersed with crumbling stations—that the world stretches out interminably like an accordion?[11]

---

10. Blaise Cendrars, *Du monde entier* (Paris: Les Éditions Gallimard, 2004), 27.
11. Ibid., 34.

However, I didn't get the same impression of Krasnoyarsk, which Cendrars oddly places after Irkutsk, when in reality the train passes through it first. Not having seen the town in a wartime setting, I was mainly struck by the majesty of the Yenisei River, the alternation of mountains and canyons, and the beauty of the taiga that extends as far as the eye can see and where the trained eye can catch glimpses of ermines and arctic foxes.

And I don't share the poet's regret that the journey became too slow after Irkutsk. I was especially moved by the beauty of Lake Baikal, whose blue and green waters of a perfect transparency seemed to be attempting to reflect the infinite, and by the limitless expanses of the abandoned parts of the Gobi Desert the train passed through as it skirted Mongolia on the final stages of its journey.

∼

In the account she gives of her father's journey on the Trans-Siberian Express, Miriam Cendrars doesn't question whether he actually made the journey, considering it a major transformative experience in the poet's early life and his "coming of age."[12]

But other more critical voices have expressed their doubts about the authenticity of the journey. The first problem is that Cendrars certainly never suffered from a lack of imagination, and the veracity of some of his movements, his

---

12. See *Blaise Cendrars*, op. cit., 24–25.

travels around Asia in particular, has been seriously questioned by his biographers.[13]

There is nothing surprising about this, given the fact that Cendrars's entire oeuvre extols the blurring of the lines between reality and fiction. This is true in his extremely romanticized biographies of Jean Calmot in *Rhum* and of General Sutter in *Gold*. The essence of his poetic activity, both in his poems and other texts, comes down to exactly this—blurring the boundaries between an unclear reality and a multifarious fiction.

On a more material level, the journey Cendrars claimed to have made on the Trans-Siberian Express could not have been without a few technical hitches. Construction on the Trans-Siberian Railway began in 1891 and was certainly almost finished when Cendrars arrived in Russia in 1904, so the route he described was theoretically possible. But, as the poem reminds us with its description of massacres, Russia was plunged into war during this period, and the railway was used only for the transport of troops.[14]

---

13. In his preface to an anthology of Cendrars's travelogues, Claude Leroy notes, "As soon as he arrived in Paris in 1912, the young Swiss poet, who disembarked from America, was accompanied by a whiff of travel, which never left him in literary circles. Understanding very well the requirements of a myth, he cultivated sudden departures and inexplicable disappearances, without neglecting to borrow a few extra trips (to China, to Africa, around the South Seas)." Blaise Cendrars, *Partir* (Paris: Les Éditions Gallimard, 2011), 10. Translated to English by Michele Hutchison.

14. Cendrars even refers to this in the poem ("In every station I watched the last trains leave/That's all: they weren't selling any more tickets"). Padgett, "The Prose of the Trans-Siberian."

If it is possible that Cendrars saw some photographs of this train, or admired it on some occasion in a station in Moscow or Paris, or even climbed on board for a brief visit, it is highly unlikely, if not impossible, given the military context of the period, that he really traveled on it, or in any case traveled on it in any way other than in his imagination.[15]

Expressing some doubt about the reality of this journey on the Trans-Siberian Express and having conveyed his skepticism to Cendrars himself, Pierre Lazareff received this famous reply from the writer: "What does it matter to you since I had all of you take it!"[16]

The humor of his response, which suggests that, like many of his confreres, Cendrars was an armchair traveler, shouldn't disguise his cleverness in realizing that the most important thing for a writer is to make his readers travel. Cendrars's poem, which is presented as the authentic account of a travel experience, certainly talks about an imaginary train, a train that can have little to do with reality. But this illusory train does correspond to the image that we might have or that we might be prepared to accept, and there is a certain kind of consistency, as with Marco Polo's China or Margaret Mead's Samoan Islands.

---

15. "There isn't a single document to show that Freddy—and particularly in such troubled times—managed to undertake such a long and risky journey. Nothing prevents us from imagining that he admired the train in the station at Saint Petersburg or Moscow. Perhaps he climbed into one of the four luxury coaches shown in the Universal Exhibition in Paris in 1900." Claude Leroy, in Blaise Cendrars, *Poésies complètes: avec 41 poèmes inédits* (Paris: Denoël, 2005), 344. Translated to English by Michele Hutchison.
16. Ibid.

What Cendrars actually manages to capture by playing on the stereotypical images attached to this mythical railway line and the original rhythm of the drawings and the words is not the authentic train as it crosses Siberia but the very essence of the train—specifically what it embodies in the collective imagination, what it represented to the writer himself at the time of writing and what it is capable of becoming for the readers he addresses in the context of a shared fantasy.

Because what the writer is interested in isn't a place in terms of geographical reasoning, but a separate dimension, a dimension that could be called *the spirit of the place*. That is to say, it isn't what he can see himself when he travels— disconnected fragments of reality or common places devoid of interest—but something intangible that only literary writing with its linguistic shifts can hope to understand and shape correctly.

As Karl May's example shows us, the spirit of the place implies a process of idealization, one that doesn't necessarily make the place better, but one in which it is refined, meaning that its main characteristics are simplified so that it can become, through the inventive power of writing, both in the present and in the future, the imaginative property of everyone.

This idealization leads paradoxically to a distancing from reality, *as though the reality of the place wasn't in the place*. The construction of the spirit of a place—we see it in Psalmànazar's accounts and those of Karl May—occurs through both a blurring of spaces and a blurring of time, transforming something into "unreality." Not only is Siberia revisited by Cendrars, but his description mixes properly Russian elements with others borrowed from countries like France, Belgium and Italy. And the journey described is simultaneously a journey through Siberia at the start of the century and during other historical periods.

It is this spirit of place, irreducible to geographic space and historical continuity, a spirit that nevertheless constitutes a profound truth, that Marco Polo grasped from his Venetian retreat, Chateaubriand through his panoramic views and Édouard Glissant in the armchair where he read his wife's accounts. And most particularly, Jayson Blair when he described a show that took place several blocks away from his office, or, in the interests of his readers, had tobacco plants grow close to an interviewee's house.

~

The text isn't only the encounter between a place and an imaginary world, it is also an *account* addressed to a reader in the context of a situation of particular discourse. If we consider, as Cendrars's formula suggests, that the only thing that counts is the reader's response, it amounts to asserting that the writer is not trying to make his words coincide with a hypothetical reality, but to adapt them to a specific space opened up by his writing where the dimension of the Other is crucial.

The spirit of place, situated in language, is inseparable from communication with the Other and cannot only be dependent on the author's imaginary realm. On the contrary, it is linked to the transitional space of the *common imaginary realm* that writing seeks to generate by taking into account the recipient's expectations. The writer attempts to give life to this place that belongs to many. It is born from his own imaginary realm but isn't reducible to it, since the spirit of place is inside him and not related to geographical reality.

This common imaginary realm is an intermediary world between reality and fiction. Characteristic of the atopic space of literature, it is highly mobile since it must be designed to adapt to the greatest possible number of readers and contexts, and, like Psalmanazar's Formosa, gather together signs that are sufficiently varied and open to interpretation to provoke reverie in very different recipients and allow them to take ownership of it.

But this common imaginary realm is also mobile in that it *constitutes a passage between the world of reality and that of fiction*, simultaneously borrowing characteristics from both. The points of reference it is composed of—which vary from one sentence to the next, or even within a single sentence—belong as much to the real world as they do to the imaginary world. The writer, like the reader, shifts constantly from one to the next.

This intermediary state between reality and fiction, of the shared imaginary realm erected by writing, creates a place for privileged traffic between these universes. The inhabitants of our world can use the adjoining character of this transitional space to move into fiction, and imaginary characters can use it in the opposite way, to infiltrate our world.[17]

The creator fosters this double circulation between reality and fiction. This is what Cendrars is alluding to when he evokes the necessity of making the reader travel.

---

17. See Pierre Bayard, *Sherlock Holmes Was Wrong* (New York: Bloomsbury, 2008).

This travel—brought about here by the interplay of associations, the blurring of space and time, and the dialogue between text and drawings—should not only be understood as image production, but, more profoundly, as a destabilization of the reader's spatial and temporal markers, capable of conveying her beliefs and psychological categories like in a dream or a delirium, and allowing the reader to pass through to the other side of the mirror.

This traffic between worlds, due to the mobility of literature's atopic space, leads us to the question of how much certain creators—just as they sometimes end up unintentionally inhabiting other periods of history than those they were born into—sometimes find themselves in places different from the ones they believe they are describing, a displacement they might not be aware of, but whose traces their works involuntarily contain.

So now it is no longer fragments of places or times that move from one work to the next—like Jayson Blair's tobacco fields or Psalmanazar's rhinoceroses—but the creator himself who finds himself transported to a different place from the one he is in the process of depicting, unwittingly importing, like a descriptive palimpsest, images that are blurred or different from those he believed he was composing.[18]

---

18. In this, Cendrars's train does not correspond—or corresponds only slightly—to any geographical location it would be pointless to try to confront it with. It is what might be called an *atopism* (the town of Honfleur with Michaux's camels or Jayson Blair's tobacco fields are atopisms), that is to say, an element of literary space which condenses several places and times and draws its seductive power from this very condensation, advancing it in the mind and thereby allowing readers from different countries and periods to believe themselves at home.

~

Saying that he managed to make his readers take the train is therefore a way for Cendrars to favor psychological presence, which doesn't imply any specific place and allows borders to be crossed, over physical presence, which primarily disrupts authentic encounters with the real and should therefore be prudently avoided when possible.

We understand how this superior form of presence in a place, psychological presence, is better than any kind of visit, which risks limiting its scope, and why Phileas Fogg, keen to capture the profound spirit of each of the regions he traversed without becoming caught up in either details or stereotypes, was well advised not to leave his cabin when traveling around the world.

Making Love

(in which we see that it isn't necessary to
go to Chicago to make love to one's
companion)

WE HAVE SEEN THAT the armchair traveler should not be
content with blurring different spaces and times to arrive at
the spirit of a place, far removed from any objective geography.
He must also show himself capable of making others cross
the permeable boundary separating reality from fiction, by
transporting them through the mirror, even if it means unwittingly crossing that boundary himself.

But he can do more than just incite them to dream and
imagine. By opening up his unconsciousness to writing and
attempting to communicate with the unconsciousness of
others, he can hope to help them to improve their own self-
knowledge, or even profit from this shared journey to repair
some of their internal suffering in the intermediary space
that has thus been created.

≈

The narrator of Nina Berberova's *The Black Pestilence*, Evgenii Petrovich, who is trying to get together a sum of money to travel to America, decides to take a pair of diamond earrings that he had pledged to a municipal pawnbroker to a jeweler. However, he finds out that one of them is affected by "the black pestilence," a flaw that deprives it of any value, leaving him without the money he needs to travel.

Then he accepts a proposal from an unknown woman who visits him at home, Alya, a professional dancer. She proposes subletting the apartment he is living in, taking advantage of their differing work shifts, an arrangement that would allow her to keep the apartment for herself when Evgenii leaves for America.

And so a strange cohabitation begins between these two alternating occupants of the premises whose paths rarely cross because of their opposing timetables. An amorous relation seems on the point of developing but is interrupted by Evgenii's departure for America, which has become possible thanks to the money Alya has given him.

Once he arrives in New York,[1] Evgenii finds work as a secretary to a tyrannical businessman, a certain Kalyagin, who, separated from his wife, lives with his daughter Ludmila. After having repaid his debt to Alya, Evgenii attempts to save money to join his friend Druzhin, who is waiting for him in Chicago.[2]

---

1. VP++
2. VP+

Ludmila, with whom he develops an ambiguous relationship, wants him to stay in New York and even expresses the desire to get married, but Evgenii, after hours of discussion and long walks with the young lady, finally decides to follow his original plan and leave for Chicago.

∾

In the conversations that Evgenii has with Ludmila, the protagonist's destination, the city of Chicago, has an essential role: that of a common imaginary realm that both of the protagonists dream of together, a place that is all the more fictional because Evgenii has never been there and can only talk about it through the intermediary of the letters his friend Druzhin regularly sends him describing the city:

> She had never been to Chicago, and she had only a vague impression of it, and although I had never been there either, I told her that once Druzhin had written to me about it.[3]

True, the letters contain enough information for Evgenii to be able to give detailed descriptions of the city to his female friend and to transport her there with his words so that they can walk around it together:

---

3. Nina Berberova, *The Tattered Cloak and Other Stories*, trans. Marian Schwartz (New York: Alfred A. Knopf, 1991), 249.

"You see it especially in those stormy gloomy neighbor-hoods that run south from the northern reaches of the river, passing by several train stations, hugging the canal on two sides and getting lost between Goose Island and the wharves. On those narrow streets, from roofs to pavements, there are staircases on the outside, fire escapes, like broken lines in the air, against a sky that is white in the day or red at night. Those stairs make you think of the reverse side of life, of buildings, of the city, they make you think of the flies backstage in a gigantic theater. Once in a while motionless figures sleep on them, hunched and hanging like black sacks, and it's as though these sleeping people hadn't laid down on the steel by chance but had battled for their sleep in a drunken brawl, or haggled for it in a drunken quarrel."[4]

Amazed by the accuracy of these descriptions that allow Evgenii to capture the spirit of the place, Ludmila asks him if he has ever been there, to which he replies that he hasn't. Evgenii then launches into a long depiction of the city's river nevertheless, entertaining the young woman to the point that four hours pass without either of them realizing it, absorbed as they are in their journey.

"People there are out on the streets day and night, as if they had nothing better to do. And they have two types of faces: some have perpetual concern in their eyes,

---

4. Ibid., 250.

whereas the others have a special sleepiness and limp-
ness. The streets run on and on until they finally turn
into notches two or three feet wide, though even then
they have names. Nothing grand or melodious, but
names just the same. Real streets there are called
Bonaparte, Goethe, Byron, Dante, Mozart, and Cicero.
But I can't tell you anything about them, I can tell you
only about the notches. These have barbershops where
tramps get their hair cut for free—the student barbers
practice their art on them . . . Besides the barbershops
there are also lots of little shops where you can pawn
things and drink up the proceeds. Once a man pawned
his wooden leg and then hopped from bar to bar."[5]

It is a place of shared imagination, then, where other
places and other times intersect, as the names of the historical
characters from all over the world suggest, sufficiently vague
in its presentation to attract the reveries of multiple virtual
visitors, including the young woman Evgenii is trying to
seduce.

≈

Despite the fact that the descriptions of Chicago extend to
several pages of the novella, becoming more and more
detailed—or perhaps precisely because they are so detailed—
Ludmila ends up experiencing some doubts about the

---

5. Ibid., 252–53

existence of the imaginary city Evgenii has become accustomed to taking her for their joint strolls:

> "It seems to me," she said, first sipping coffee from her
> cup, then cutting up a pear with a knife and offering me
> a small piece on a fork, "that there is no Chicago. Wait,
> let me explain it to you. There's a strange, scary,
> immense city that you know a lot about but that neither
> you nor I will ever see. Instead, it's as if you and I both
> were already living there."[6]

Ludmila isn't unjustified in being perplexed about the reality of Chicago, in any case the Chicago to which Evgenii takes her regularly without ever having been there himself. The reader actually learns some time later that Druzhin, the friend Evgenii was supposed to join there and who is furnishing him with the information, only exists in his imagination, and he has been inspired in his description of the city of his dreams by letters that don't exist:

> I don't know who to write to first: Alya or Ludmila. Alya
> asked me to write about myself and how I was getting
> on, which would be an awful lot easier to do. Ludmila
> asked me to write about Druzhin, and that's very hard.
> She must have guessed that there never was any Druzhin,
> that I dreamed him up, that I was going without knowing
> where I was heading. To nowhere, to see no one.[7]

---

6. Ibid., 255.
7. Ibid., 273.

The fact that Druzhin doesn't exist doesn't in any way prevent the narrator from confidently going off and looking for him, convinced that the search itself will bring Druzhin into existence. He feels that their correspondence has somehow paved the way for this encounter:

> I'd do better to spend my evenings walking the streets and searching for Druzhin—he has to be somewhere after all! I got so used to the idea of him that maybe I actually will find him in the end. I can see him clearly before me: reddish hair, thoughtful, a little sad, a white spot on his forehead, a thick mane of hair. We would have something to say to one another, something to discuss.[8]

Everything happens like this, the boundary between reality and fiction having been crossed, as though the shared imaginary realm that Evgenii has constructed with Ludmila has served as a conduit for a virtual creature and allowed it, by following the opposite route to that of writers and readers who lose themselves in texts, to emigrate to our world and materialize in it.

∾

At the end of the novella, when Evgenii has finally left Ludmila and arrived in Chicago, we discover that his difficulty in

---

8. Ibid., 274–75.

finding a place to live relates to a dramatic experience he once had in France. He had passionately loved a woman during the war, and she had died in his arms during a bombing, while they were making love:

> Her whisper. Her moans. Her sob. Her cry—and one more. At that very second—a deafening thunderclap and the six-story building began to rock. The sixth and fifth stories flew up in the air. The fourth and third crumbled to earth, and the last two shuddered for a long while, sprinkling us with sand and plaster from the ceiling. Her eyes were still closed and two tears fell from under her eyelids, two tears of final bliss.
>
> Then the cellar ceiling started to give way, but not the walls. Deafened by thunder all around, I tasted plaster in my mouth, going down my throat . . .
>
> They came with stretchers. My love. My life. Mutilated. Silenced.[9]

The invention of the imaginary city of Chicago—an atopic and achronological place that it would be pointless to try to match up with any real location—had thus allowed the narrator, incapable of starting afresh at any fixed abode, to grow used to the prospect of living there one day, while he simultaneously invented the consoling character of a companion capable of welcoming him to the city the day he did go and live there.

---

9. Ibid., 272.

But this invention also allows him to begin to map out his original trauma and to look for ways to repair it. In the town constructed by his imagination, he doesn't only try to discover a physical location but also a psychological one by reliving the moment of drama, a primal scene close to the one Freud talks about, in which a fascinated child is horrified when she comes across her parents having sex. It is a painful reunion with a repressed past marked by suffering, all the more difficult to reach, no doubt, because it carries echoes of the infantile scene.

So the narrator is led to invent for himself a compensatory city, responsible for making up for the shortcomings of his own existence. This ideal Chicago, where pleasures are free and disagreements appeased, had been rebuilt in a way that symbolizes the extinguishing of conflicts and a harmonious relationship between its inhabitants:

"You can take a walk in the park and admire nature, you can listen to a wind orchestra in the city parks for free, you can find an old newspaper and read it from cover to cover, old newspapers being more interesting than new ones. You can compose a ballad and sing it on some corner and people will listen to it all the way through— that's just how people are. You can attend free courses to learn which mushrooms are poisonous and which aren't, and when the Australian aborigines devised a calendar."[10]

---

10. Ibid., 257.

More specifically still, when you pay attention, you see that whole swathes of Chicago are composed from scenes that have marked Evgenii, like the incident with the pawnbroker at the beginning of the novella. Abandoned objects, for example, become playthings that children granted total freedom can just pick up in the new city:

"You know in Chicago there are children," I said, watching the shores slip farther and farther away from us and the air darken, "who don't steal, don't beg, and don't sell their bodies. They play cards, day in and day out. . . . They set themselves up in a vacant area, where a building has been torn down, on a pile of rubble, put a collapsed legless couch there, or bring an old mattress from some nearby dump, and gamble around the clock for four, sometimes five days."[11]

What Evgenii describes here with his Chicago is certainly an imaginary realm, but more than that it represents a projection of his inner landscape, that is to say, the spatial part of his unconscious with its contours and fault lines, where the opposing forces that he is attempting to reconcile clash. It is a landscape under construction, whose spaces are no longer menacing but, on the contrary, reassuring in their reworked form:

"Their only pleasure is in choosing where to sit. Here, if you want. There, if you want. And choosing where to

---

11. Ibid., 263.

sleep: in the night shelters there are sleeping cells on two levels, and they're all identical so far as I can tell, but they choose all the same. The cell locks from the inside. They can hook the latch from the inside, you understand, not from the outside! They can also choose what to eat: kidney beans, peas, green beans, sweet corn. No one is forcing them. Each one has his own jar, not an official ration, but of his own choosing, individually eaten, protected by that latch. His own bed and his own jar."[12]

The vague plot of land where the children play and the cage which can be opened and closed at will, allowing elderly people to isolate themselves, describes an inner landscape that is certainly still devastated, but in the process of being restored, and which can, as such, appeal to the imagination of the woman to whom he provides his description. She finds herself invited, by bandaging her own wounds, to come and share it.

~

In fact, if the narrator starts to find a psychological place here, and not just a physical one, it is not only because he allows the repressed trauma to resurface in himself as it is healed, but also because the very way he behaves in his invented city opens up a path to others, thereby making a romantic relationship possible:

---

12. Ibid., 262.

I'll live again and see whether something comes of all this, after all. Even the dead are resurrected so why shouldn't I, as I'm alive? Only for that I had to do something, I had to make a decision, get moving, adapt, I had to invent cities, people, sorts of stories, my own life, fit in, walk in step, try to resemble other people. And it had to happen quickly, otherwise I'd turn into a vegetable.

I'll definitely write to Alya. She would have slept on my shoulder, lying in my arms, whereas I would have slept on Ludmila's shoulder—that's plain as day to everyone. I'll write to her, too.[13]

A place of individual projection and psychological healing, this virtual Chicago is also the intermediary domain of a romantic relationship, which isn't conducted through physical exchange but through this imaginary journey undertaken together. As in the case of Blaise Cendrars, the travelogue is a way of transporting the other, including in an amorous sense. This is because the connection of inventing a communal ground as the two protagonists do is a metaphor for the physical relationship they aren't yet capable of engaging in, handicapped as they are by their pasts.

Like the two protagonists of George du Maurier's *Peter Ibbetson* (1891) who, prevented from ever coming into physical contact with each other since one of them has been imprisoned for life, find each other at night in their dreams, Chicago

---

13. Ibid., 274.

offers a transitional space where Evgenii and Ludmila can meet and learn to live together. The space is doubly transitional since it is the intermediary between the two friends but also serves as a conduit between the traumatic sexual act and a future one.

But this imaginary Chicago doesn't exclusively serve to express the romantic relationship between the two protagonists through transposition. It also helps them attempt to discover a singular identity and as such functions as a kind of *shared inner landscape*. For these two uprooted beings, unable to find a place to live or a person to live with, the imaginary city of Chicago is a way of communicating with each other by surveying an invented territory together:

> "You know, Evgenii Petrovich," she said after a while, "with you I feel quite different. No one would ever recognize me now. It's because you're not in the least bit afraid of me. You can't imagine the happiness when someone isn't afraid of you."[14]

This search for a shared inner landscape is symbolized in the novella by a boat trip. One evening, Ludmila suggests to Evgenii that they drive down to the furthest tip of the city, head seaward and make a tour of the island. Once they have embarked, they are no longer sure of having taken the right boat, and soon find themselves spatially disorientated:

---

14. Ibid., 258.

Three ferries were docked, ready to sail, and we boarded one of them and immediately were struck by the care-free feeling you have when you're sailing without knowing where or when you'll be back: a rare feeling, to which you can almost never afford to succumb.

"Maybe we should ask where we're going anyway?" I said when we had sat down in the wicker chairs, and the boat, having sounded its horn and let out a cloud of black smoke, began moving away from shore.

"It doesn't matter. It's too late now."[15]

And so the two protagonists take a double journey: a real journey around Manhattan Island and a virtual journey through a common inner landscape, constructed as a site of psychological sharing where they can be together to discover themselves and each other.

This shared inner landscape is not founded on elements of the real world that serve as points of reference for their discussions, but on shifting elements of the unstable schema employed by literature. In this way, the disorientated boat trip taken by the two protagonists comes to symbolize their wanderings in the atopic space that their mutual reverie invents in order to try to heal their wounds.

≈

15. Ibid., 260.

How do you construct a common inner landscape for another person or for multiple readers? By inventing this realm, the narrator of *The Black Pestilence* manages to talk about himself to the woman he loves, opening up a place for her in his discourse. The inventive power of shared travel is due to it being both profoundly individual and resolutely open to the Other. As such, it is mainly a linguistic place that cannot be located in any concrete geographical space.

The invention of this fictional Chicago—unsuitable both in space and time—is typical of literary writing in terms of its relationship to the world. It forsakes real points of reference for atopic elements and falls under what might be given a contradictory term, a *plural singular.*

The description of Chicago is assuredly singular because the person giving it has never been there. The scattered elements of Chicago that the narrator has been able to collate from different sources are associated here with intimate memories. This association gives rise to an eminently subjective vision of the city, which is above all a projection of an inner landscape.

But the woman recognizes herself in this personal description of an invented territory, so much so that she is capable of moving around in it with her companion in her imagination. Our narrator, therefore, invents a particular form of singularity in which the privileges of personal creation do not prevent the fantasies of the Other from being welcomed without injury and the creation of a shared reverie.

The form needs to be precise enough for the reverie to be

able to latch onto it, but at the same time, sufficiently open to the imagination for the Other to recognize themselves in the landscape and make it their own. If we say that literature is written in the plural singular, this also implies that in order to write about the world, the writer starts from the most personal, but looks for linguistic forms likely to speak to others because they express something of *universal experience* through him.

In this respect, Evgenii's gesture could be interpreted as a symbol of literary activity in as much as it looks for a route toward others that passes through the most intimate parts of the self. Having access to the self enables you to make the Other travel and to stage an encounter between inner landscapes—an encounter and a shared inner landscape where the unconscious of each person enters into dialogue with the other to invent a symbolic shared place in which each person attempts to reconstruct themselves, like in a fulfilling romantic relationship.

~

And so it is in talking to the other about yourself, and not about real places—just as Marco Polo did to his beloved and then all of the world's readers—that you are best equipped to both know them and have others discover them. What makes a good traveler is an ability to pass through geographical places in the knowledge that each of them contains a part of yourself and can open up a path toward others, as long as you are wise enough not to stop anywhere along the way.

The invention, in any written or spoken context, of an appropriated place is all the more credible if it is borne along by the truth of its subject. You should listen to yourself most of all, and devote yourself to writing and the reconstruction of the self if you want to attract others to your inner landscape through a universal experience.

Epilogue

THIS BOOK HAS AMPLY demonstrated that getting to know cultures that are different from our own doesn't in any way require physical movement—far from it. The armchair travelers described here were gifted with common sense and decided not to venture far from their homes. Still, they didn't let this prevent them from giving detailed descriptions, often passionate ones, of places they hadn't been to, which, nevertheless, had put a stamp on their existence.

In fact, they observed that there are some risks attached to sojourning too close to the field of study without taking in that view of the whole that Phileas Fogg or Chateaubriand claimed to be the only true way to travel. A physical journey certainly allows us to see the place we are visiting in the optical sense, but it doesn't allow us to see it in depth, in relation to the immense atopic space of which it is just one tiny element, or with regard to the eternity it is a part of.

Alongside the risk of proximity, there is a further risk—that of stability. Truly understanding a place and attempting to express the nature of its universal value requires grasping it in its dynamism, that is to say, in its possibilities for development within the discourse in which it is captured, addressed to a particular audience that must be seduced and carried away by language.

Faced with these two risks, nontravel doesn't mean remaining immobile. On the contrary, the places we conjure up in our imaginations can allow us to travel within ourselves, and it is this journey to the inside of the self, made with company if possible, that mobilizes the armchair traveler, attentive to the things that foreign cultures can offer him and that he, in turn, in his desire to make the world known, transmits to others.

∾

Knowing the benefits of observation from a distance presents another significant advantage, relating to reading great works of literature, which can be appreciated in a new way once the veil is lifted and the truth is finally told about the circumstances of their creation.

It would be a logical assumption, given the many people who have practiced observation from a distance, that the number of armchair travelers is significantly greater than one might think. We should be highly circumspect about all of the books we know, starting with the various forms of autobiography.

Since it is likely that a traveler as respected as Marco Polo didn't get any further than Constantinople, are there any writers essential to our knowledge of the world we shouldn't reread from this new angle? Aside from those who have acquired a solid reputation as armchair travelers, like Chateaubriand or Blaise Cendrars, it is probable that numerous authors enjoying a serious reputation have used similar techniques with impunity.

However, prudently rereading the most famous authors doesn't in any way imply that we should challenge their accounts—unless one falls prey to the illusion that the closer you get to a place, the better you can know it. No, it should be about knowing how to appreciate their accounts in a different light, no longer just for their documentary value but with all the poetic and heuristic power they possess to invent possible worlds.

～

Taking into account the atopic character of literary space has yet another effect, the consequences of which are not insignificant. If the uncertain limits of this space lead many writers to consciously visit the places in their minds without physical travel and to take their readers there as well, why not imagine, conversely, that fragments of the world of varying significance outside the work don't also manage to transport themselves there on occasion, without even the author's knowledge?

How can we avoid asking ourselves, when reading literary works and faced with certain atypical descriptions of towns or landscapes, with certain representations of unusual physical traits or clothing that don't correspond to the place described, whether certain parts of different worlds from the one the writer honestly believes he is describing haven't slipped into the work without his knowledge?

And, taking one step further, can't we go as far as to ask ourselves whether certain writers don't just unwittingly welcome into their oeuvre fragments of distant universes but also travel themselves to other cities or countries without realizing it, thus describing places they cannot imagine finding themselves in?

Studying the various forms of this spatial mobility and remembering that works are constructed on moving ground opens up unknown spaces to scientific exploration, present and active in their authors' works without their knowledge, whose still living traces, hidden behind seemingly innocuous descriptions, it would be good to take stock of.

∼

So, looking further than these first few examples, it would be useful to found an *atopic criticism*, whose mission it would be to complete the study of the temporal mobility of works[1] by way of their spatial mobility and to better grasp the movements that secretly animate them behind their apparent deceptive stability.

It would be a form of criticism that would draw on all the consequences of the permeability of the boundaries between the space of the work and real space and would take an interest, for example, in that mode of circulation that allows literary characters to immigrate to our world on occasion,

---

1. See Pierre Bayard, *Le plagiat par anticipation* (Paris: Les Éditions de Minuit, 2009).

or the writers and their readers to immigrate, like the armchair travelers in this book, into the world of the work.

This form of criticism should also draw attention to the communication between the spaces in different works— which on closer consideration really only form a single space devoid of boundaries and thus common to all travel— and study the way the characters sometimes move around between works without respecting the visible borders.

It is likely that Immanuel Kant sensed, or even secretly theorized, about this spatial mobility between literary works when he obstinately refused to deviate from his path, trusting in his imagination and writing skills, and convinced that even during this promenade past known places, he had more chance of meeting others than in any journey far from the self.

Lexicon

Armchair traveler: A person keen to know other cultures but who chooses to explore the world by staying at home and using their imagination.

Atopic criticism: A type of criticism whose object is to study the specific spaces produced in literature and art.

Atopic space: A space produced by literature and art, characterized by the permeability of boundaries between works and the world, as well as between different works.

Forgotten place: A place you once went to without remembering anything about it.

Imaginary realm: A fantasized and idealized representation of a place, like the island J. M. Barrie invented in *Peter Pan*.

Informant: A person, living or dead, responsible for informing the armchair traveler (see above), either because they live in the place the latter wishes to describe or because they are capable of making the physical journey to the place to prevent the armchair traveler from having to take any risks or becoming exhausted.

Inner landscape: A spatial representation of the unconscious. The inner landscape occurs when the subject projects herself onto surrounding places, transforming them into imaginary places.

Literary truth: A type of truth different from scientific truth that is founded on noncompliance to the traditional categories of space and time.

Nontravel: A way of traveling characterized by a loss of control over the locations and a dispossession of the self.

Observation from a distance: A type of observation advocated by this book consisting of staying well away from the place you wish to study.

Original place: A fantastical representation of the primary sites of childhood, marked by omnipotence and the immediate fulfilment of the slightest desire.

Participatory observation: A type of observation advocated by the writers of the Chicago school, consisting of immersing oneself in the environment that one wants to study.

Physical presence: The type of presence in a place or an environment requiring the presence of the body.

Place one has heard others talk about: A place you know from external sources, like books or informants.

Plural singular: The process by which the writer uses personal experiences to communicate with the greatest possible number of readers.

Psychological presence: The type of presence in a place or an environment not requiring the presence of the body.

Real place: The most objective possible representation of a place, necessarily distorted by the work of the unconscious that substitutes for it an imaginary place.

Spirit of a place: The essence of a place, irreducible to its contingent appearance at any particular moment in history, which attempts to grasp writing by going beyond objective geography.

Universal experience: An experience shared by living persons in specific places and in different periods.

Unknown place: A place you know nothing about.

View of the whole: A synthetic vision of a being or object that doesn't stop at the detail but attempts to grasp its deep essence, going beyond appearances.

Visited place: A place you have made a quick trip to.

A Note on the Author

PIERRE BAYARD is a professor of French literature at the University of Paris 8 and a psychoanalyst. He is the author of *Who Killed Roger Ackroyd?*, *How to Talk About Books You Haven't Read*, and *Sherlock Holmes Was Wrong*, among many others. He lives in Paris.